Allison Vale has written more than a d[...] betray an unhealthy curiosity with obs[...] of the lives of women in history, such as *The Lost Art of Being a Lady*, *How to Push a Perambulator* and *Amelia Dyer: Angel Maker*, a biography of the murderous, 30-year career of Britain's most prolific baby farmer. She lives near Bristol with her husband and their two children, and though she has not yet read anywhere near enough of Virago's backlist, she's desperately hoping her Caitlin Moran obsession more than compensates.

Victoria Ralfs discovered a borderline inappropriate ease in discussing life, love and relationships with her secondary school students early on in her career. This gained momentum in the field of learning disability, where she wrote, spoke and trained nationally and (occasionally) internationally on Sexuality & Relationships Education. Her husband and two, now adult, children have happily and healthily survived the Velcro penises in their study in Bristol. Victoria's wider family would probably describe her as an 'annoying, gobby do-gooder type', hence her desire to include them unflatteringly in this, her first book.

Other Robinson titles

Taming the Tiger Parent

365 Steps to Self-confidence

Stress-Free Feeding

Growing Up Happy

Healthy Eating for Life

How To Raise a Feminist

Allison Vale and Victoria Ralfs

A How To Book

Robinson • London

ROBINSON

First published in Great Britain in 2017 by Robinson

1 3 5 7 9 10 8 6 4 2

ISBN: 978-1-47213-708-1

Typeset in Times and Sabon and Gill Sans by TW Type, Cornwall
Printed and bound by CPI Group (UK) Ltd, Croydon, CR0 4YY
Papers used by Robinson are from well-managed forests and other responsible sources.

MIX
Paper from
responsible sources
FSC
www.fsc.org   FSC® C104740

Robinson
An imprint of
Little, Brown Book Group
Carmelite House
50 Victoria Embankment
London EC4Y 0DZ

An Hachette UK Company
www.hachette.co.uk

www.littlebrown.co.uk

How To Books are published by Robinson, an imprint of Little, Brown Book
Group. We welcome proposals from authors who have first-hand experience of their
subjects. Please set out the aims of your book, its target market and its suggested
contents in an email to Nikki.Read@howtobooks.co.uk.

For Pammy and Rops, my Raising Agents. You really were staggeringly inappropriate and wonderful. And you are still EVERYWHERE.

Vik

For Mum and Dad, who raised two of the FINEST women I know. Even though neither of us can jive. Or sing all the words to 'Hen Wlad Fy Nhadau'. Sorry about the swearing – Vik made me do it . . .

Al

Contents

Acknowledgements

We have plundered recollections of the lives and stories of many to write this book and could not be more grateful to have known/ worked with/been related to such extraordinary people. And thank God for them because my, there have been some eejits! We've learned just as much from them about how it all rolls too, though, so we're thankful, truly . . .

Huge admiration and thanks to those women and men with whom we haven't had a gin (in person, like) but whose humour and bad-assery have given us the most edifying, hilarious and hopeful soundtrack, especially when writing this book: Nina Stibbe, Sali Hughes, John Niven, India Knight, David Bowie, Sandi Toksvig, Rob Delaney, Matt Haig, Laura Bates, Brené Brown, Lena Dunham, Sharon Horgan, Amy Schumer, Lauren Laverne (*especially* for 'The Pool'), Caitlin Moran and of course, the ultimate broad, Nora Ephron.

We extend enormous thanks to Giles Lewis and Nikki Read at How To Books, Little, Brown for taking a punt on a pair of pals with a lot to say. We are so very grateful for your faith in us and for your enthusiasm for this book – and for endorsing the swearing.

We are indebted to the men and women who have been unfailingly patient with our discussions around this subject for a whole six months – you know who you are. Special thanks too to Beth House and Kirsty Bradley-Law, two extraordinarily busy and inspirational human beings, who nonetheless found the time to read our book and offer words of encouragement. And to Julie Barclay, for her encyclopaedic knowledge of all things theatre.

Special thanks from Al to all the mates – the women who have (sometimes unwittingly) been my testing ground for much of the past six months: Claire, Lynn, Carolyn, Al, Beccy, Debs, Paula, Jacks, Pen. An extra thanks to Pen, for giving me the key to her home to use at will whenever mine was too filthy/chaotic/cold/full of teenagers for me to be able to work. Thanks for your generosity, clean house and well-stocked fridge.

To Mike, Tom and Louisa – endlessly supportive, relentlessly tolerant and absolutely the nosiest, sweariest, hungriest, LOVELIEST family I could ask for. Thank you for letting me use so many of your moments.

And to Vik, Barker to my Corbett; Cagney to my Lacey. This was fun, let's do another!

From Vik to Rach, Lou and Ness – massive thanks for your love, friendship and belief in me. Mand – the authentic one, my extraordinary sister, the keeper of the Loveridge story vault – you have been so supportive of my writing, love you so much. Al, without whom I wouldn't be anywhere near having started to write, let alone having a book published. Thank Christ I found you, mate, cause I no longer have to feel weird! Let's get rich and piss off the batshits.

Really Small Gang

Josh and Beth, I hope this book isn't too embarrassing. I burst with love and pride at the people you have become and thank you from the heart of my bottom for putting up with all my nonsense. Kev, we done made good ones, didn't we, babe? I love you so much and am massively proud of what we cooked, us four, with added cats, @21.

Prologue

Al

Vik and I became colleagues three or four years ago, working as educational consultants in the field of Learning Disability. The first time I heard her train a room full of primary school teachers she used the words 'blow job' in the opening minutes. I knew *on the spot* we were going to get on. Very quickly, we became mates, fuelled by our mutual love of talking, an inexhaustible opinion on *everything*, her shameless capacity to remain sober until the fourth glass and my shameful inability to keep a secret after just one. The genesis of this book took a little longer, and was probably crystallised thanks to Vik's recounting of a conversation about feminism she'd had with the regulars in her local.

Feminism, we came to realise, is a word so many ordinary people never actually use to describe themselves. We're happy to label ourselves 'religious', 'Corbynite', 'atheist', 'climate-change denier', 'Pisces'. . . But 'feminist'? It seems folk will still go to enormous lengths to distance themselves from that word. Which is weird, frankly, because when you unpick it, the building blocks of feminism are basically all *the good bits*, the stuff any parent tries day after day to set up for their kids.

We're talking about stuff like,

Respect, for yourself and for others.

Confidence and self-belief to aim high, to persevere, to deal with failure.

Empathy to see that others are basically just trying to get through every day as best they can in the circumstances, whatever those circumstances look like for them.

A healthy understanding of the rules (and the guts and sass to know when to bend them).

And, naturally, underpinning it all, one basic truism: that we are all *equally* fascinating, *equally* valuable, *equally* capable of altruism, *equally* able to change the world for the better. *Of course* we are.

That's feminism, isn't it? And it's what every parent wants for their kids . . .

. . . every parent that's not a dick, that is.

So, it dawned on us that maybe we are *all* feminists, but we don't all like the word yet. Maybe the challenge we're faced with now is to persuade people to feel as good about the word 'feminist' as they do about words like 'Friday', 'carbohydrate' and 'annual leave'. And *then* it dawned on us that we're totally the kind of women to rise to that challenge. So, before we start, take a look at the conversation Vik had with Kirsty and Chris, over that fourth glass. Once you've read that, take a look at the book they inspired us to write.

Cheers!

PS From Vik –

Al can't drink. She's not lying – it was almost a deal-breaker for me, to be honest. But then we spent our first two hours on the road together and I realised I had found my spiritual twin because frankly, there are few people who feel as I do about sausages. Also, as it turned out, we share a philosophy about pretty much everything else on earth.

So, I was in the pub one night . . .

Parenting, Persil and a Portuguese Mix-up:

Vik

An evening in the pub with Kirsty and Chris, parents to Devon (eight), Michaela (five) and Lewis (eighteen months).

What does feminism mean to you?

K: Don't know, really. It's like even though I get that it's about equal pay and that, I wouldn't say I was a feminist because I don't hate blokes or anything.

C: I s'pose I better be careful how I answer that, right? Well, I don't know if it means anything to me other than women who are annoyed. To be fair, in the past there was a lot for 'em to be pissed about, but I'm not sure any of that's true now.

K: It's not just about getting the vote, Chris.

C: I'm not saying it is, but what is there left that a woman can't do?

K: But we still have to put up with a lot of shit.

C: Kirst, you don't take any shit from *anyone*, love!

K: Not from blokes, no, *I* don't! But *women* do, on the whole. I don't know if this has got anything to do with feminism or sexism or whatever but what gets on my tits is the papers. It's always about famous women and how they've got old. No one cares less about Michael Douglas and Sean Connery and all them. They can be the wrinkliest bastard on earth but all the papers talk about is the women's plastic surgery and tits. *Always* about tits! I'm so bored of that.

C: Yeah, I think that's true, to be fair. I have a look at it but there's always more about the birds' looks than the blokes'.

K: You're just saying that, Chris, to sound a bit intelligent cause Vik's asking you the question.

C: No, I'm not actually. Women get judged on how they look more than blokes. It would be stupid to say that wasn't the case. But in, like, the workplace, I think it's a lot different now. Look at you, Kirst – no bloke in this pub would dare speak to you in the way they talk to other women. They respect you.

K: Chris, that's because I'm in charge and if they start trotting out any crap, I shut it down! But when I was in my twenties it was a lot different.

C: What do you mean? You've always been scary!

K: Fuck off! Chris, you've no idea. The sort of men who come in here who you think are really good blokes are the same kind of blokes who would call out to me in the street when I was younger. All like 'Get 'em out for the lads!' That goes on *all* the time. Now I'm in my forties I would tell 'em to sod off, but back then I was too scared cause I've had friends that gave the wrong look back and got harassed. One got beaten up and left by a skip behind Asda.

C: Those type of blokes are pricks.

K: Those types of pricks are everywhere, Chris, and they will still be there when Michaela is fifteen.

So, on that then, what does feminism mean for both of you in how you parent your three?

K: I don't want my boys to be that kind of bloke. And I want Michaela to get to where I am now quicker than I did.

C: There's no way our boys would do anything like that.

K: Tell the truth, Chris, have you ever catcalled?

C: *No!* Well, not seriously – I mean maybe at school to the girls – but that's not the same. Michaela is like you though, she won't put up with it.

K: That's not the point though, is it? I think she has been around enough women who don't put up with all that. Strong women, like your mum and that. But the boys shouldn't think it's OK to behave like that in the first place. It's time that changed, but trouble is, they are all over Facebook all the time, saying stuff about each other. I am dreading ours going on there.

C: Well, we'll have to be strict on it, won't we? Michaela, she's a ball-breaker though, love, like *you*! I'm not too worried.

K: D'ya know what, Chris? That pisses me off. What does 'ball-breaker' mean? It's the same as all that 'high-maintenance' shit I hear across this bar. Men don't get described like that and to be fair, a lot of the blokes I know are bloody high-maintenance!

C: In what way?

K: In that they can be so needy. They expect to have a mother as well as a wife. They are dead selfish and I don't know, it's like they think the world owes them something. Women are expected to make their lives as easy as possible just because we are 'lucky' to have them as a partner. It's bullshit, when I think about it. I love blokes – some of them are my best friends and I like the laugh you can have with them in the way you can't with women but I don't think any of 'em are *better* than me! Even though I'm pretty sure that's what *they* think. I don't want Michaela to ever feel like she's less than the boys, or that she should do the housework while they sit on their asses.

C: Ha, like that's going to happen in our house – I do everything!

K: On account of the fact that I earn twice what you do, Christopher, and do more hours. I am not coming upstairs after a twelve-hour shift in here and ironing your fucking socks!

C: I don't expect you to; I never have. So I don't think the kids will think that's how it s'posed to be. Lewis *likes* doing washing. He gets the Persil out and says, 'Daddy, wash?' Perhaps he'll be gay.

K: *See*? That's what I mean. For Christ's sake, Chris!

C: What?

K: A little boy likes helping out so he's *bound* to be a poof! That's what I am saying. All right, in our house you do stuff because

I'm at work but if you start talking like that and well, what if one of the boys *is* gay? So what? I don't care!

C: I don't care either, Kirst.

K: You say that cause Vik is here.

C: Fuck's sake, Kirst! No, I'm not. I knew a kid at school who was obviously a gay and he was given such a rough time. In the end he topped himself. I went out with his sister – she was lush. His mum never got over it. There's no way I would want Devon or Lewis to go through anything like that.

K: Well, if you mean that then you've got to not say things about bloody Persil and that then.

C: Yeah, well, all right.

Do you think you do anything different in how you parent Michaela and the boys?

C: No, I don't think so.

K: I don't know, I think we might – I'm not sure, really. They want to do different things. Actually, I'm not sure if they always do. Devon likes all sorts, not just football. He likes books.

C: He's good at footie, he's just doesn't realise it yet.

K: Oh, I get it! He doesn't know he's destined to play for England. Christ!

C: No, not that – he just lacks confidence. It will come, though.

K: Michaela's already confident . . .

C: I *know*! It's great. In the play at school, she was mint!

K: Not just that, though – she played football in the Algarve with all those local kids, didn't she?

C: Yes, she did, and I'd had a few beers and I didn't realise it was her cause you'd scraped all her hair back and yeah, I know, I didn't make enough fuss.

K: You thought she was one of the boys and then when she scored a penalty, you looked almost a bit upset.

C: I wasn't upset, love – it's just not what I expected to see. I want her to do whatever she wants – you know that.

K: Point is does *she* know that?

C: She's *five*, there's plenty of time!

K: Well, you say that but if you put her off doing things like football, she might just not bother and it's the same with the boys.

C: What is?

K: What if Lewis wants to do ballet?

C: S'all right by me.

K: And if the blokes in here started taking the piss?

C: They wouldn't.

K: *Really*? John Matthews wouldn't go, 'Chris, mate, your boy the next Darcey Bussell, is he?'

C: I wouldn't bite.

K: You'd be embarrassed, though. And you wouldn't stick up for him.

C: I'd *try*, Kirst.

K: You would have to, or I would kick you in the nuts. And then I would kick John Matthews in the nuts!

C: You don't like him anyway so it would be a good excuse.

K: No, I don't like him but he spends £400 a week in here so I think sclerosis will get him before I do – I'm just watching it happen. He'll be paying for Lewis's tap classes! (They look at each other, and then laugh really, *really* hard.)

What do you want for your kids?

C: I want them to be like their mum.

K: Oh, you soppy *shit*!

C: Nice!

K: I want them to be happy. That's what everyone says though, isn't it?

C: Because that's what all parents want, isn't it? I'll tell you what, though. Thinking about what you're sayin', though, Vik, and all of that stuff, I think that I *do* want something different for ours. I mean, they will know how to work hard and all that because everyone around them works hard. I won't tolerate them doing anything else but it does drive me mad how vile people are to each other, and I know women get more than their fair share of that. That needs sorting out. I don't know if that's what feminism is, but it's fairer.

K: I feel like that. It's just about fairness really . . . Get me a gin now, please, Chris!

(He goes.)

The Mix Tape used to mean so much in pre-digital days. A declaration of love, a desperate apology or an attempt to look achingly cool as you wedged in a 'very rare piece of Kraftwerk'. These compilations meant so much to the maker, as they hoped they would lift or light up the recipient.

So we have included some tunes here and there with that very same hope. Soundtracks to stories old and stories still unfolding . . .

Introduction: Why Feminism?

Al

Growing up in the 1970s and '80s, feminism scared me. I felt like the feminist movement was an exclusive club for irritable, intimidating women and that membership would require me to be stridently angry – about *everything*. I would be called upon to hate men, read Virago's entire backlist and refuse to shave.

It wasn't for me.

In any case, I didn't need feminism, I told myself. I was getting by on the strength of my own graft. Gender wasn't going to be a barrier.

That wasn't actually how it turned out. At the age of nineteen I started to get sick. I was an undergraduate, away from home, but I could deal with it; I would go to a GP and get it sorted. No problem. The persistent, peculiar jerks that every morning sent my breakfast flying across the room, or had my legs suddenly collapse from under me, were passed off as 'psychological' by my GP, who wrote me off as 'nervy'. Jesus, I thought, I'm sicker than I thought if I'm making this stuff up! He referred me to a clinical psychologist, who supported his diagnosis. *For a year.*

Until the day I had a full, *grand mal* fit in public and an A&E doctor diagnosed Juvenile Myoclonic Epilepsy. (I could have kissed him; I grinned when he told me.)

The same GP had me unfasten my bra every time I saw him so as to listen to my heartbeat. *At every appointment*, no matter what I went to the surgery for. I was nineteen; I wore under-wiring: I didn't question it. He was a doctor and I'd never listened through a stethoscope. Yes, it made me uncomfortable, but who was I to question?

At twenty-one, I made my first foray into the world of work – sales and marketing in the City. I was greeted by Zachary, a gorgeous, pin-stripe Adonis, born and raised in Chelsea, sporting Filofax and red braces. That first morning, he interrupted his meet-and-greet with me to make a phone call. He called a colleague from a higher floor, telling him, 'I'd say she's around a seven or eight.' I guessed he was talking about me. The 'seven' stung: it was the first day of my career, but the 'seven' was what lingered.

Nine years later, I was a secondary school teacher, working as a head of department in an academic London school, when I gave birth to a beautiful son with Down syndrome. Towards the end of my maternity leave, I made a phone call to my Head, asking to switch to a job share so I could spend time with my baby working on vital early intervention programmes.

The Head: young, fierce, single, childless. Female. She gave me her answer without pausing for consideration. 'No, job shares invariably fail within education and you have a lot on your plate now,' she told me. Her implication was that as a new mother, particularly a new mother with a learning-disabled child, I wouldn't be able to deal with the emotional drain of home life at the same time as the demands of middle management. Maybe she's right, I thought. She must be: she's very experienced.

Of course, she wasn't right. Neither was the GP or the clinical psychologist. I just didn't have the tools to express the injustice I felt in those situations.

So here's the thing: feminism needn't be radical. It isn't necessarily strident, angry or hairy. It's about justice, self-awareness, guts. It's about *respecting* the authority and experience of others but it's not always about *accepting* it. Certainly never at the expense of what you know to be true and just. And it had been the missing link in my story.

I wasn't able to see any of that until I was a mother myself.

Feminists aren't a niche interest group – they're decent, courteous, respectful members of your community. They party hard, work hard and know better than to dish out any shit, or to take any of it from anyone.

That's everything I want for my children.

Vik

I grew up on a council estate in South Bristol in the 1970s. To survive there as a child, you had to show real prowess for the street game British Bulldog, which was essentially a mixture of running and violence. Girls were tolerated as long as they were perfectly happy to play the position of cheerful casualty.

As the charge began, I would head for the legs of Peter Denford ('Denford Nylons', as we affectionately called him and his brother, after the crimplene emporium of the day – Brentford Nylons. To this day, this makes me laugh out loud. Sorry, Peter!). I figured I could duck and hurl myself clearly through Peter's arched thighs as he squatted, ready for the oncoming onslaught.

I was always catastrophically wrong. Instead, I would end up face first in Bristol City Council gravel. But not end up in tears though, because then my brother would be mortified and I would be consigned to squash duties.

I was seven. The boys were in charge. When Lee Morriss pulled my pants down for a look, the parents all around cooed and said, 'Aw, first love . . .' Those were not enlightened, safeguarding days.

Women of the street cooked, cleaned and discussed the chief topic, which I recall was the varying amounts their men drank and their respective responses to these patterns of imbibing. I remember, without any apologies for romanticised, soft-focused nostalgia, being blisteringly happy.

I was the youngest of four, three girls and a boy; we had massive freedom and were loved and ignored in equal, happy, healthy proportions.

Alsatian dogs, Chopper bikes, homemade taffee apples and bonfires . . . Holidays to Jersey – fourteen people crammed into a Mk 2 Cortina on the ferry from Weymouth. Guest houses where you had a choice of fruit juices for a *starter.* Man, exotic or what? Daytimes we were allowed to burn to a crisp on the beach, sail practically to Guernsey on our two-foot dinghy, and then be dried off and bundled back to get ready for going out for the evening entertainment. These spectacular nights out were about the *men.*

'It's our time now,' my Uncle Dave would claim, which was interesting because I don't recall his days being exactly *crammed* with rock-pooling, walks and games of tennis with his children, but there. Variety shows in clubs called 'Blue Lagoon' that featured the singing talents of 'Miss Sandy Gold', who always opened with a Tammy Wynette number and was hot from a cruise around the Balearics.

The men stayed at the bar all night. Meanwhile the women would be at the 'family' table with children of all ages, some already asleep, others skidding on the dance floor in their socks and some going for an illicit drop of Double Diamond under the tablecloth, egged on by the dads, who would do us all the great honour of popping back every now and again with crisp mountains. The whole purpose was for the men to drink steadily until the bitter end. And then someone would pass around a six-foot blow-up bottle of champagne and we would all pose with crispy, melanomic smiles for a photo.

It was *BRILLIANT.*

In 1976 we moved to an area of the city close to the university, where I encountered some folk who might as well have been a different species. After passing the Eleven Plus, I arrived at Fairfield Grammar School and made some interesting new friends, who invited me round for tea.

Their families weren't like ours. My mate Lynn Cox and her brother Neil called their parents by their first names. This scared me: I wasn't entirely sure if they were actually her parents at all, but I didn't like to ask. I was also terrified of their use of words like 'appropriate' and 'fundamental' – I thought they must be from Portugal, or something. In my house, we said things like ''Iwat', or 'I'm not having the *green* Penguin' or 'Shut *up*, your mother's programmes are on'.

Food at the Coxes was also a revelation: honey, *brown* bread and casseroles from heavy earthenware dishes that had what I later found contained (oh, the glamour!) olives. Over dinner, Lynn's dad would ask his wife what she thought about things that had happened on the news, or how she was doing at work. My jaw must have dropped in awe at this (possibly revealing an olive).

Then they played the piano. In about three hours I went from terror to lust: I wanted the Coxes for my own. They'd been to India and they had jars with couscous in them. I didn't know what couscous was, but it looked really intelligent. I told my brother about them and he said 'Bloody hippies'. But I felt I was simultaneously entranced and alienated. Not because they were seductively bohemian and clearly intellectual, but because the rules that the women and the girls of the house lived by were nothing I recognised. How come they were so different?

The word feminism: I never once heard it as a kid. What I did hear around me were strong, extraordinary women being summarily dismissed by the men around them and those men being treated like heroes in return. When we gathered together with other families, the men were always served first; the biggest chop, the best roasters. I don't recall any grown-up woman around me having a career or a dream of her own. Certainly not any dream she talked about; not that extended beyond white goods or package holidays. They sure as hell weren't downtrodden, not all of them anyway, but they were resigned to something I couldn't see clearly or understand. I knew enough to know I didn't like it, though.

At fourteen I meet the man who will go on to become my husband – a gentle, quiet chap of nineteen. He has a car; very quickly he has my heart too. By sixteen, with no one talking about university or careers, and my sister having her babies, I went to work in a payroll office. We got engaged, had a party and spent £46 on a ring. By seventeen, we had bought our own house and by eighteen I was married. It's what people did, there was no other narrative, and I fell happily into buying peach festoon blinds and learning how to use my deep-fat fryer.

We had friends, one couple in particular where the guy was an unspeakable misogynist. I started to challenge his sense of entitlement, his cutting me off mid-sentence – I was really starting to mind this shit. He laughed at me. I was labelled, affectionately, as a bit 'gobby'. I swallowed it down – I knew I was more intelligent than all of these men but I had nothing like the guts to challenge it. It would make me unpopular, less attractive; that wouldn't do. I'd never seen a woman behave that way, and still be liked – and I really, *really* wanted to be liked.

1989. The Open University. Holy crap, what a revelation! What untapped joy and discovery. All of the clichés around learning that are clichés because they are so joyously *true*.

And then I'm pregnant: a miniature Elvis in a plastic fish tank. I'm days from twenty-one years old. He is magnificent and something (not him any more) is turning inside me. Then, 1994: in the middle of the night, in my own bed, in forty minutes, my daughter . . . Urgent, annoyed and then serene. For about five minutes . . .

Six months later we are in the pub, it's summer and my babies are enjoying the sun. A friend of the family, a bloke, I mean, a *BLOKE*, passes me by as I walk to the ladies'. He looks at my breasts, then my face and says, 'Yeah, I like 'em big.' I've had twenty-five years of hearing this stuff. And I go to smile, wearily, appear to be flattered and not be difficult, as is expected in this tribe.

Then I look at my girl in her pram, and again at him and say, instead, 'See, Lance, you don't get to say that to me. Because you see, it's not OK. You don't get to look at parts of my body, decide if you like them and then tell me about it. It's not a compliment. And it's probably why, at thirty-seven, you are still single. Mate, stop it . . .'

It had taken years of accepting the small chops at the dinner table and more than my fair share of *Bulldog*, but finally, after two babies, I'd found my feminist – and she was here to stay.

I want my girl to do LOADS . . .

I want her to love and lust after people but not define herself by those people.

I want her to be free of my neuroses, bad habits and hang-ups but also to know that 'not perfect' is the only way to be truly happy.

I want her to worship me (if I'm honest).

I want her to be angry about some things, do something about them in her own way, but still have a massive laugh about all of it and then listen to Neil Diamond with me for a bit.

I want her to enjoy her body: paint it, dress it, cherish it, throw it around without care on the dance floor. I want her to relish all her feminine powers but know they are hers to decide how to use and with whom.

I want her to enjoy (and mostly feel a bit sorry for) men. As mates, as colleagues, as lovers if she chooses, and to be kind and expect kindness back.

I want her to believe that being a feminist actually just means all of these things and is the best gift I can give her.

I want my boy to be a MAN, not a BLOKE . . .

I want him to understand that 'man' does not mean he has to be macho – because that's all bollocks. Nor does it mean he has to be afraid to show fear, pain, compassion and kindness because these things make a good, real person, irrespective of genitals.

I want my boy to have adventures. And text me photos of (some of) those moments, adding 'You would LOVE this!' even when, clearly, I wouldn't.

I want my boy to hug his nan/aunt/dad/sister/uncle until he winds them – and not give a shit who is watching.

I want my boy to love without fear and with his whole heart. I want him to like, love and enjoy the women in his life — and the men too. And approach the whole game with respect, empathy and enormous fun.

I want my boy to love his home; here with us, and then with whomsoever lights him up and makes him feel similarly safe. He'd best come home and watch South Park *with me and eat chimichangas regularly, mind, or I will KICK OFF.*

I want my boy to look at what society says he should enjoy and be into, smile, and then do his own thing. If it's macramé, I will stock up on the jute. If it's Ultimate Fighting Champion, I will stock up on the Valium. Either way, I want him to show up in his own life — I will still take the Polaroid for Nan.

I want my boy to know and celebrate women for all the same reasons he admires men and not be afraid to say that out loud, in a common-sense fashion. I want my boy to be a feminist because it wouldn't occur to him to be anything else.

Chapter 1

'Not From This Factory'
Raising our tolerance: we are all feminists

Al

Recently I read a blog entitled 'Why More Mothers Aren't Feminists'. It took me a while to get past the title. The tsunami of twentieth-century radical feminism carries sentiments like this in its wake: motherhood, with all of its domestic drudgery and career breaks, is death to feminism. As lately as 2012, French feminist Elisabeth Badinter published a book called *The Conflict: How Modern Motherhood Undermines the Status of Women*, in which she condemns attachment parenting for 'tethering women to the home'. Babies are one thing, but stay home a while to raise them? *Unthinkable* . . . Badinter is entitled to her point of view, naturally, but as far as we're concerned, it's *bollocks*!

That kind of stuff is damaging, divisive and disruptive. Strident judgements such as these can leave us all, mothers and childless alike, with a nagging sense that our lifestyle choice is somehow less than acceptable. It can put too many of us on the defensive, convinced we are somehow in *conflict* with other women over our lifestyle choices. And none of that's OK.

We've all done it: we've all given way to self-doubt and given in to the need to find a goat to scape at some point in our life. And we need to cut it out.

I am reminded of an evening some years ago; an uneasy encounter with a woman I imagined to be on the 'opposing side' of this alleged conflict. With hindsight, I see my mistake: I mistook her poise and focus as the exclusive badge of the blissfully childless woman. I imagined her free to luxuriate in herself, digging deep into bottomless pockets of energy and drive, while my own pockets were holding bays for tiny plastic stilettos, Penguin wrappers and used tissues, the detritus of my brood of small humans. I saw how unrecognisably *different* her work-focused, child-free life appeared to be from mine, and crucially, I thought I saw those shortcomings for which I judged myself, to be fabulously absent in her.

I didn't *know* her, then; I imagined her. And I found myself horribly lacking by comparison. Indulge that delusion and it's a small step to the place I ended up: *she loathes me*, I decided in the first few moments of our encounter. And then, within a half-hour, self-defence: *Fine. I'm not much liking you, either.*

So, we're clear, then: *this is not an encounter of which I'm proud.* A decade on, I can't even be sure this is how the encounter played out, but it's certainly how it has festered in my head ever since.

I sat in a shabby-chic urban pub with a theatre crowd after a preview performance of a show at a provincial rep. Me: an educated woman, a successful educator and a published, jobbing writer in my late thirties. Although I didn't know it on this particular night, I was also on the verge of becoming a theatre journalist. I'd been to see the show because the female lead was a mate of mine and I joined her afterwards in the pub, sipping bourbon with the rest of the cast and crew. Significantly, I was the only parent in the group.

Holding court, with a dancer's easy posture, was the show's young director. It was quickly apparent that this wasn't a woman to dilute her attentions: she concentrated her piercing gaze on just a single member of her audience, effectively excluding the clutch of people pressed around her. I should have recognised this upfront – a form of tunnel vision I've often seen put to use by under-confident adolescents, a way of blocking out the many in order to hold their nerve in a crowd. Instead, I decided this woman oozed precisely that kind of self-assurance that tips easily into abrasive disdain.

The conversation was a hot debate centring on the destruction of a bird in the evening's performance. The moment, she informed us all, had been overplayed. The frustration the actor felt in that moment had been pushed to the brink of farce with the result that the audience felt permitted to laugh when the bird's neck was wrung. That wasn't what she wanted of the scene: she wanted to shock.

She suggested instead that the actor wring the neck of a live bird every single night for the rest of the run. (I kid you not, she genuinely expected stage management to procure a live songbird every day, two on matinées, to be slaughtered before a paying audience. For three months.)

Clearly, this was lunacy. And, frankly, her self-contained allure was already making me edgy. So as I sat, caged in on all sides by actors, former actors, rising stars and fallen ones, I decided to brave an opinion of my own. I suggested that the audience might not be laughing because they found the moment funny, but because they felt incredibly uneasy in the face of such disregard for life. They might even be seeing *themselves* reflected in that action. Not farce, then, but a moment of valuable connection. Empathy . . . Much more powerful than shock.

Pleased with how this had sounded, I leaned back on my perch, brushed the hair out of my eyes and reached for my bourbon.

My lovely old mate offered up a generous, 'Interesting . . .', but the rest of my audience had grown silent, staring alternately at their pints and their director. With a brisk intake of breath, the director broke the silence, her faux-sympathetic glance lingering in my direction for just a moment before uttering a definitive: 'They *will not* laugh at my bird!'

I suspect that in that moment, everyone present realised that from now on, no one would be laughing.

I loosened the sweat-soaked scarf from around my neck (the one I had almost believed I had tied with panache earlier on, but which now felt like a noose), and drained my bourbon.

Crushed, I lingered at the bar, enjoying the cold pressure against my midriff, stifling hot in oversized pants I hoped were acting as a stomach-wall substitute and aware as I was ordering that no woman (least of all a twelve-stone 39-year-old) ever looked good on a fourth bourbon in an hour and a half. But hey, I'd managed three and nothing terrible had happened.

I watched her play havoc with the lie of men's pants, throwing back her head, tripping through the arpeggio of her laugh, while seductively and oh so subconsciously stroking the white underbelly of her exposed neck.

And then someone made a joke – something derogatory about 'breeders' and motherhood. And someone else asked was she 'tempted to sprog'? Ha! As if someone like her would ever risk the varicose veins and fold-over stomachs of post-pregnancy. It was laughable and I failed to stifle a snort.

She tossed out a dismissive 'Children? Not from this factory!' and her gaze alighted on mine, momentarily taking even my breath away. The next remark she pitched my way before sniggers had died in fawning throats.

'But I do envy you. While I'm grubbing about in theatreland, trying to carve out a living, you're so *sorted*, aren't you? You have your *children*! How many do you have, did you say?'

It was pregnant with judgement and I swear I could see laughter dancing in those eyes.

I blinked back tears of rage (I despise that in myself: rage lets me down when I need it most, leaving me with nothing but ineffectual sobbing, like an errant wench thrown across John Wayne's lap). How dare she step out of her world and trample on mine, I thought. How dare she pretend she knows the first thing about success? *Real* success. The kind you truly appreciate when your child lets go of your hand to walk through the school gates for the first time. How dare she give out that she understands the first thing about carving out a life, a *real* life – the kind that comes clawing its way out from between your thighs, screaming to be heard, and held and loved.

And that's when I decided there was nothing elegant or graceful or poised about this woman. What she had wasn't beauty: she had artifice. And I had seen enough.

So I took a great, open-mouthed gulp of my fresh bourbon and pictured myself striding across the room towards her, drenched in a spotlight while fawning theatreland looked on. I imagined reaching her, holding her stare, my eyes swollen with psychosis, hers beautifully amused. I would look beyond her mocking eyes, perfect cheekbones and rosebud mouth. Away from the face – down to what? The *chest*! Flat, barren, incapable of comfort.

I would throw back my head and laugh (and make no mistake, I'm laughing here only in the fantasy ending to this encounter: no quantity of bourbon would have made me confront a beautiful woman). Five Jacks and Cokes and suddenly the way to assert my own bounteous femininity would be staring her in the face. With a grin, I would choreograph a nifty pas de deux of my own, whipping out sagging, stretch-marked tits from their amply under-wired brassière and snuggling that pretty little face of hers in the yeasty dead centre of my plentiful bosom, with a triumphant, 'Babies? Count 'em!'

Course, that's not what actually happened.

In the pass-agg, real-life version of this encounter, I didn't give her an answer at all, but was rescued by my lovely old mate, heading outside to suck up lungfuls of cigarette smoke third-hand from her fag (I don't smoke but I'm a perversely enthusiastic passive smoker), while she steeled herself for the next instalment of the unresolved bird question and I tried not to cry.

Ten years on, I wonder was the director being derogatory about motherhood *at all?* Or was I hearing a tone that wasn't there, the product of nothing more than my own insecurities and three too many bourbons? Was her timing indicative of nothing more sinister than her sudden, uneasy realisation that there was a *parent* in the room, (where generally, in her world, there were none?) Was my outrage far more to do with where *I* was than where she was?

With hindsight, it seems likely. No matter. In any case, that night was bigger than the sum of its parts. If that young director was lashing out at all, perhaps it was at the very thing I'm about that she felt maybe she *ought* to be about too: motherhood. I had done *precisely* the same thing, of course, only in my case it was her bristling feminine prowess and that had left me wanting to hiss and spit like an alleycat.

Granted, I did all of my lashing out psychotically, privately, whereas I had imagined she had given public voice to hers, buoyed by home-turf bravado. She had dipped into the command she had over those around her, I'd decided, to deride me with simple small talk. I just went home, comfort-ate Doritos and drunk-wrote myself a cathartic scene in which I subjected her (and in true self-deprecating Vale fashion, simultaneously also *myself*) to a whole other kind of public humiliation.

The point is, the whole episode left me with a lingering malaise. I wonder if she felt it too? I had a suspicion that I was somehow 'lesser' for calling a halt in my career to have children. Was she lying in a hotel room, dousing out her biological clock with a New World Sauvignon and lonely tears, wondering was she right to pursue other priorities?

The enduring myth of a feminist conflict can leave any of us convinced the *other* woman has the upper hand in any given encounter. The truth is, there *is* no upper hand, only individual women wading through the quagmire of their own messy adulthoods. There are *no* conflicting paths when it comes to motherhood and feminism but there's *everything* wrong with perpetuating a culture that demonises women for dragging themselves along a path that's different to yours.

So, I regret the secret scorn I poured on her that night on account of her commitment to her career. I regret having quietly judged her for making the choice to eschew motherhood. I would even forgive her if she had, in fact, poured her public, taut-limbed derision over my choice. I don't, however, regret disliking her apparent lack of avian sympathies, although thankfully common sense would finally prevail in that respect. And I don't apologise for finally going to print with my private vision of the perfect, peculiar comeback. And all of that's OK, because here's the other thing: you can *still* be a feminist and bitch about other women, but maybe that's another book.

> *I was always too self-centred and irresponsible to have kids. I know that never stopped many others, but I am a narcissist with a conscience.*
>
> Debbie Kasper

SO . . .

Before we go any further, let's throw out the old Feminist Rule Book. It no longer applies. The new rules are: there are no rules. All that matters is that you're kind to yourself and that you step up whenever you sense that others aren't showing you, or anyone else, that same kindness.

Now that you're heading into parenthood for the first time, take a moment to remind yourself what's great about you. Not to satisfy any flaky, hemp-clad, inner-goddess urge, but because it matters. Once that baby drops into your world, there's a fairly hefty chance it will take over your every waking thought. A swell of emotion, a tortuous, elongated spell of sleep deprivation coupled with enforced gin-prohibition means you'll be at significant risk of sidelining the things that make you you for a while. What takes over is baby. It's useful upfront to remind yourself what matters to you, what makes you a thinking, feeling, vibrant person, and keep a tight hold.

So, what are the mantras by which you live?

First, let's get the mood right. Don't be tempted to hit Charlene for a bit of 'I've Never Been To Me' or Christina Aguilera's 'I Am Beautiful (No Matter What They Say)': we need something celebratory. She can keep her 'discontented mother'/'regimented wife' thing to herself. Let's step it up: Chaka Khan, 'I'm Every Woman'. And turn it UP!

Try answering these questions honestly:

♦ What earns your respect?

♦ What fires you up, makes you feel most impassioned?

♦ What motivates you?

♦ What pisses you off?

♦ What gives you the biggest sense of pride?

♦ What makes you cry?

♦ What makes you intervene, step up, shout out, help?

♦ What fascinates you?

♦ What absorbs you?

These are some of the things that influence how you feel about, respond to and behave around others. They also shape how you treat yourself: they are what's you about you.

Knowing what matters to you is important because right from that little blue line, the societal pull to begin motherhood perfect and get better from there on in is ENORMOUS. We all do it: we get sucked in by all the other voices – the mothers, sisters, medics, guidebooks, Oprah . . . And we end up in exhaustive pursuit of the perfect diet, or of the Mozart concerto most likely to have Foetal-Me hit genius from the off.

A million different voices, all of them expert, all urging you to dampen your instincts and do it their way.

Resist!

The unavoidable fact is that you won't be the perfect mother – who is? But listen: you don't need perfection. And more to the point, your baby won't need it from you either.

Think about the people you treasure most in the world. Invariably what keeps us anchored to these people is their gloriously flawed, complex, real selves. We don't keep them in our lives because of whatever version of perfect they let the world see on their Facebook status. So keep a hold of all that about yourself. Keep liking that about yourself. And keep working on all that. Because that's all our kids need from us too.

Pregnancy is a time to chill. Enjoy getting a seat on the bus. Take lovely long baths and eat loads of hot dinners (trust us, it'll be months before you'll do either again). And keep doing what you're doing. Because you don't need to figure out what perfect is. You will be good enough – you're already good enough.

> *Sometimes I just pick her up and stare at her, and I realize, my only job in life is to keep her off the pole.*
>
> Chris Rock

Chapter 2

'The Good Wife's Guide' becomes 'Team Home'
Raising a family of equals

Vik

'Is he 'avin' a cuppa tea then?' my mother would ask, itching at the sight of my husband, in from work for now bordering on four minutes and without a brew. More pressingly for marital harmony, *I'd* failed to ask him if he wanted one as soon as he stepped into the room. This was not her script and she looked about as comfortable as the artist Grayson Perry in chinos and a polo shirt.

'Perhaps he will have one when he starts making dinner,' I counter ever so calmly, smiling conspiratorially at him as his face falls into recognition at the familiar scene. 'Nanny, would *you* like a cup of tea?' he would ask her as he stepped across the room to hug her and she would *MELT*. I mean literally, Wicked Witch of the North styley pool on the floor (without evil and child hate, natch).

For her, our Team Mum and Dad way of living was equally baffling and beguiling. She would say, regularly, with an enormous swoon in her voice 'Oh, he's so *GOOD*!' Because any man who did something around the house other than take out the bins or wash the car was a creature of whom she had no experience. In his defence, my late father did go to Tesco a whole twice in his last years. So it would be fair to say I had me a plan when it came to casting off some stitches from the fabric of my childhood experience of domesticity: I was gonna be doing something very bloody different to a life judged largely by the quality of my whites. My mother considered slightly greying towels as a *MASSIVE* character flaw, once remarking on observation of a neighbourhood washing line, 'She is a *dirty* bitch, that one! It's no surprise to me she's on her fourth husband. *AND* she got they guinea pig things. For Christ's *sake*!'

I married a man who, despite his own very traditional patriarchal upbringing, just assumed we would divide up the chores because, well, why wouldn't you? There'd be more time together for things like telly, carbohydrates and well, *other* things. (Note: make the most of when your kids are little and they GO TO BED EARLY, I beg you. After the 12.5 seconds it takes them to get to adolescence, downstairs evening sex becomes as likely as David Cameron becoming CEO of Amnesty International.)

I can't tell you the JOY then, when my 2-year-old son developed a passion for vacuum cleaners. His toy Electrolux – 'The Um' – was his constant companion and even though the pretendy ironing board and iron was largely staged by me for a photo, it was THERE, in among the cars and Duplo and all the standard 'small person at work and play' kit. And Daddy was there, just as likely to be seen with a garlic press or a mop in his hand as a hammer.

Was it effortless, getting into this rhythm of sharing the load, sending out the loud and proud message to our children: 'No outdated gender defined roles in OUR gaff, babies!'? Well, no, because life is often hard and unpredictable and we're flawed. But we kept talking about what we wanted it to look like. I have always loved Robert Louis Stephenson on marriage:

Marriage is one long conversation, chequered by disputes.
Two persons more and more adapt their notions one to suit the
other, and in process of time, without sound of trumpet, they
conduct each other into new worlds of thought.

In the now infamous *Good Wife's Guide* featured in *Housekeeping Monthly* of May 1955, wives of the day are urged to consider advice such as, 'Speak to him in a low, soothing and pleasant voice'; 'Remember he is master of the house, you have no right to question him'; and my particular favourite, 'Put a ribbon in your hair'. I have naturally curly hair. On some days, I look like Miriam Margolyes on speed. A ribbon would make me look like a splendid bovine success from the Bath and West Country Show.

Clearly, in 2017, we know this 'advice' is utter bollocks and has no place in modern relationships and families. What then, has replaced it, in our thinking and in our homes? Is there anything of value to take from the era of *Mad Men* apart from the amazing use of table lamps?

It's 2006. I am running a national team for a voluntary organisation. I'm away a fair bit – in exotic places, like King's Lynn. I have delivered three days' training back to back in Derbyshire and I fall into my car and onto the M1. It is February. All kinds of knackered, I am tearful for home. I stop for coffee and it's PISSING down. There are hold-ups everywhere and I can palpate utter despondency in my fellow motorists as we cast sideways glances at each other below our gantry sign generals. One trucker salutes me, and I do it straight back, like it's an entirely expected exchange: we are soldiers of asphalt. Finally home, as I take my key from the ignition, I look in the rear-view mirror. I look like a charity campaign poster: 'Text FUCKED to 55555 to give this woman back some kind of hope'.

I can see steam in the kitchen window and the outline of my fella: this means food. I drag my sorry arse to the door and it's open so I tumble in. He comes around the corner.

'Let me get to the loo, I need to pee and I look like utter SHIT,' I say.

'This is indeed true. Shit hot,' he laughs.

The audacity of the lie, the brilliance of its timing, makes us both laugh and we snatch a 'hello' kiss.

The boy (now sixteen) is suddenly there.

'That's rank. Mum, where are my football boots?'

Dad: In your cupboard

Boy: Mum, can you drop me at Gaz's later?

Dad: No, she can't. Walk.

Boy: Mum, you look like shit, man! Sit down, he's made curry.

Thing is, through our own unique conversation, we have made a home where as long as bodies and surfaces are fairly clean, that'll do. We are not slobs – I can't bear the 'Oh, I'm FAR too preoccupied with reading about TTIP to dust' garbage. Spray a bit of bleach around, you lazy bugger! I am also actively scared of people who have minimal interiors when they have kids in their life. To me that's just joyless and unwelcoming. A clean, warm home is a glorious thing for everyone from eighteen months to eighty years old. And it's achievable by people who have penises too, which is incredible really, isn't it, considering there's no one with hair ribbons to cheer them on?

I would no more rush to the bathroom to freshen up on hearing my husband's car than he would suppress a much-needed burp. Who could *live* like that? But we take care of each other, ourselves and of our home: differently, equally, but not slavishly. We hand each other a glass of wine, supper, a clean shirt, depending on what's going on right in front of us in that moment in our lives. Sometimes we run a comb through our (ribbonless) hair and spray a spot of Ted Baker on because we fancy each other and want to keep on doing so. Occasionally (less so now we're middle-aged cause we've largely nailed the ongoing convo), we can be heard to yell 'Are you SHITTING me?' on sight of an unloaded dishwasher or a terrifying bank statement. Sometimes, too, we even talk to each other in low, soothing tones.

I cast back on then from my own childhood and we knitted a new family blanket that holds us all safely and cosily. It's a bit frayed in patches but oh boy, enough of the sewing metaphors now!

> *If your kid needs a role model and you ain't it, you're both fucked.*
>
> George Carlin

SO . . .

♦ It still amazes me that often women of my generation, and younger, still take the burden of domestic responsibility despite working a full-time job like their male partners. The research keeps telling us this is the case. STOP IT!

♦ Kids need to see fairness and kindness hand in hand – 'You're knackered, I'll make tea. It's my turn anyway'. It's not a favour if the man takes in the washing, it's his washing too. It's about who has the time to do things, around work and everything else. Period. Work it out and stick to it.

♦ I have no idea how we send the right message around work and gender equality unless we start here – and mean it as we go on. I know some really sensible and intelligent people who have paid unintentional homage to the 1950s with this narrative in their homes. They now wonder why their 18- and 20-year-old sons think housework is none of their concern and are talking about girls in less than respectful tones. Make the footprint early on.

♦ Fess up time: I've found it hard to entirely cast off (oops, sorry!) what my mum did and the ridiculous guilt that I can internally manufacture if people don't have the full range of clean pants. I've not been nails on this from the get-go – I can very easily do too much for my children because I want them to have the sense of home and nurture that I myself enjoyed. This environment is very possible though, but it needs multiple players, including the kids themselves: both genders. When you're on your own, this is incredibly hard. Read columnist Sophie Heawood on single parenting – she is quite brilliant.

♦ Relationship maintenance is essential. Raising a feminist is about bringing up robust, respectful kids. And all the while we are working out how to be robust ourselves while respecting those closest to us. It's all a work in parallel and in progress. It is absolutely no good to devote all your energy and headspace to getting it right by your kids when the relationship you are in, that they live in too, is not being looked after. Remember, it's about who we ARE.

♦ So, take time in whatever way is physically and financially possible to regularly create space for you as a couple. It's extraordinarily restorative to take even an afternoon to hang out together and really talk. Otherwise it's snatched moments over the top of kids' heads and often the stuff that ideally gets worked through without them listening.

Belle and Sebastian – 'Perfect Couples' – cause we all know these folks. They seem to have it all down, right? Nah, they don't! Brilliant video. My parents had that VERY rug.

Chapter 3

'Wonderful Nipples' and Other Insufferable Doctrines
Early motherhood: Raising your self-belief

Al

> *I quite liked having a baby – I think I won't put it more strongly than that. But I had no intention of allowing motherhood to disrupt my work as an archaeologist.*
>
> **Mary Leakey**, Disclosing the Past

At the age of twenty-eight, I stumbled, bewildered, into a loosely planned pregnancy. I'd been working as a secondary school teacher in North London for six years and was already a middle manager. I loved teaching, loved the students, loved my subject and, for the most part, I loved the other teachers. I was ready for more; the question was, what? A career progression – take on a bigger department? A faculty? An MEd? . . . Or a baby?

Motherhood still seemed an impossibly grown-up adventure but somehow, once the idea presented itself to me as an option, it took roots and refused to be shaken off. It took just two months to get pregnant. I'd taken folic acid by the truckload and read every manual and advice column out there. I cleared out the spare room, filled it with baby-gros and muslin squares and became obsessive about eating my greens: I was ready.

All the more bizarre, then, that arguably the biggest decision facing first-time mothers was something I hadn't given a second thought. Pregnant and nursing mates had brought it up: *breast is best* was thrown in my direction on more than one occasion. But hey, it was leafy, middle-class professional North London; the NCT Army was resident in every coffee shop. I tucked the question away, aware that the very thought of getting my baps out in public felt laughably, excruciatingly embarrassing. Plenty of time to decide all that . . . Anyway, I'd been bottle-fed – it was the thing to do in the 1960s and it hadn't done me any harm.

Four weeks ahead of schedule, I took delivery of the smallest human being I had ever laid eyes on. At just 4lb 6oz, he was, as my fabulous midwife told me, 'Tiny! But he's a tough little bugger!' An hour later, she also told me they thought he might have Down syndrome. Turned out she was right – on both counts.

Breastfeeding, I discovered while still on the ward, was something everyone was vehemently keen on. But each time I tried it left my son raging and hungry. I was shit at it, I decided, unaware that his extra chromosome would be impacting on his muscle tone, making the act of latching on far harder. I scolded myself that I could neither grow a perfect baby (actually, he *is* perfect, I just couldn't see it yet), nor feed him as nature intended. Stung by the guilt of motherhood from those earliest hours, naturally I felt wretchedly sorry for myself.

The midwives on the ward recognised that my son and I needed help. They hooked me up to a machine resembling the early code-breaking monstrosities of Bletchley Park. Huge and blue and noisy as hell, it hurt like hell too.

A long line of strangers appeared at my bedside to advise me, or observe me, or dangle my tiny son face-down over an outstretched palm in order to observe his low tone. I spent a lot of those first three days sobbing.

And then in walked a Breastfeeding Advisor. Vast and American, she talked with a permanently cocked head in a loud roar, as if new mothers were universally deaf and stupid. In a confessional tone, she said she had heard I was having trouble feeding my baby and proceeded to help herself to a look at my tits.

'Oh!' she exclaimed in what sounded like astonishment. 'But you have wonderful nipples!' Her pronouncement tailed off into silence, leaving me to complete her thought trail: *So what's your problem?*

I exploded – I wanted motherhood, I wanted to enjoy my baby, I wanted to get to know him, figure out what he needed, and do my best to give it to him. But I wanted everyone else to piss off out of my business. I'd had a skinful of strangers studying my nipples, pinching them, trying to shove them into my son's tiny mouth.

So I told her to leave me alone to bottle-feed. I needed to do something easily. My caesarean scar hurt like hell and so did my boobs; my son's chromosome test was looming and worse still, so was his heart scan. He was losing weight and turning yellow and I just wanted to feed him in peace.

In her unfalteringly tilty-headed, patronising Californian lilt, she said, 'That's OK. You're *allowed* to bottle-feed.' But nothing about the woman reassured me that she meant it.

Some hours later, I was still sobbing when another new mum from the ward appeared at the end of my bed, clutching her perfect, sleeping baby girl. Eighteen years on, her name eludes me, but she and I had been fully paid-up members of the self-titled Pre-Eclampsia Long-Stay Residents Group, admitted for several days prior to giving birth because of high blood pressure. She was from Manchester and was reassuringly secure about her right to call all the shots (carrying her baby while walking around the ward, for instance, rather than wheeling her around in a cot as insurance policy dictates).

I unburdened my feeding-counsellor trauma. She was livid: 'Fuck 'em, love! He's tiny and your tits are massive. I'm using Aptamil – I've read up on it. They reckon it's the closest to breastmilk there is. Bottle-feed him! Fuck 'em!'

Of course I knew that breast is irrefutably best for baby, yes, but it felt hopelessly out of my reach. With hindsight, I see that breastfeeding is *not* best for baby if it comes at such an emotional cost that it leaves the new mother reeling with inadequacy, a blethering mess, unable to function.

Dangerously close to blethery, I blamed myself, for all of it. It was only two and a half years later when my chromosomally typical daughter latched on like a pro within her first few moments of life (and more or less refused to let go for the next thirteen months), and only then did I realise just what an insurmountable challenge my mammaries had presented my little boy with.

And only then did I realise why I had been right to get angry with that Feeding Counsellor that day. Her job should have been to help me understand my tiny hungry human being, to make sure I realised there were reasons why we were both struggling to help him feed, and that none of those reasons were our fault. To bring me the kind of specific feeding advice which enables mums and newborns with Down syndrome to breastfeed successfully. And then, having armed me with just the right amount of information and understanding, to back off and leave me to make my own choice, free from blame or judgement. Real choice, real support . . . But that's not what she did. She left me battling a sense of failure; a sense of having fallen at the first hurdle motherhood had thrown my way. *Mea culpa.*

So I bottle-fed my son from that day on and though I didn't ever fully shake off the guilt, I was grateful for it. Bottle-feeding enabled me to function as he needed me to, and with every feed, I fell a little bit more in love with him. He grew strong and healthy and exceeded everyone's expectations and shattered more than a few stereotypes, growing into a fine, confident, fascinating young man.

So many times over the past eighteen and a half years have I remembered my fabulous Mancunian maternity ward inmate at the Royal Free in Hampstead and felt an enormous, teary-eyed swell of gratitude. I'd been made to feel wretchedly imperfect by a woman who just wasn't getting it, but at exactly the right moment my lovely mate held open the happy, happy door to 'Good Enough'.

That's sisterhood!

SO . . .

This is where it begins: right now in those early days and weeks, heady with exhaustion, when you can't imagine yourself being anything other than completely welded, physically and emotionally, to this small person. The thing to hold onto is this:

♦ Raising a strong, independent kid will always be more about who you ARE than what you do.

♦ You will make mistakes, who doesn't? But you will be enough.

♦ Our children are not meant to be ourselves. They are not meant to repeat us, fulfil us, affirm or absolve us – that's not their job. They are meant to be themselves. And so are you.

> *A lot of mothers will do anything for their children, except let them be themselves.*
>
> Banksy

Don't fuse your identity with your child!

◆ From the kick-off, even if it's just moments within this talcum/puke/ tear-stained and scented stage, take time to be yourself. And that's hard when you are feeling, 'I can't even take a shit without this kid, how am I supposed to think about Syria? Or sex?' But read the paper if you want to; think about something that isn't, 'How many ounces now, Dave?' or centile charts, or the uncanny ability of your health visitor to crush you with a LOOK.

◆ Not everyone feels straight away that early surge of emotion for their baby. Exhaustion, self-doubt, pain and pethidine are a heady mix all on their own. Add in the vagaries of postpartum hormonal mayhem and the net effect can be that it can take a while to feel the swell of maternal bliss everyone talks about. No matter. Breathe; be kind to yourself. There is no 'normal' when it comes to these early days of motherhood. Go through the motions, talk, get help, be patient but don't panic: the love will come. Honestly, it will come.

◆ Filter advice. Now, more than at any other time, sage-filled words will come tumbling in from every angle. Hopefully, the real sisterhood will show up: the women who will say 'Pour water over your stitches as you take your first poo, love' (excellent advice, especially when followed by 'There's a lasagne in the oven and I've brought more gin' and even, 'Isn't that Nigel Farage a cock?').

◆ It helps to have a ready-to-roll line to hand. When the neighbour/ aunt/mum-in-law wades in with the nuggets of wisdom, smile, nod warmly and then trot out something like, 'Yeah, I might try that. I guess we are going to have to see what works for us, because there's no rule book, is there [insert name]? I mean YOU know that, right?' You need something that gently deflects interference while reminding folk that they were once where you are – baffled and battered and ever so slightly tired of advice. But tread gently: you might need these allies later down the line and it'll make it easier for you to say, without violence, 'Mmm . . . I might not start lifting him onto a potty at night at six weeks old, Jean, to be honest. But thanks. Fancy babysitting next week?'

♦ Non-broody friends can be huge allies in those early days; mates who are at different ages and stages to you, not just the fellow lactators. Most will love a bit of a coo-fest with your baby but there will be days when you really need to be around people who will steer the conversation onto something else. Or offer to take you to the pub. Lap that up!

♦ You will feel under enormous pressure to make certain choices right now, and breastfeeding is probably the most emotionally loaded of them all. Of course we all know the benefits. We understand all of that and most women want to have a go. If you love it, wonderful! If you don't, that's fine too! You've got years of guilt ahead so don't get bogged down over this – your precious energy has better places to go. Bottle-feeding is absolutely fine if it's the best fit for you, your baby and your world.

♦ Remind yourself you don't need to be perfect, just good enough. And then feel good about being honest with yourself. Your tiny speck of marvellousness is still too wee to get that you're being strong and assertive over these tough choices, but all the same listening to your inner voice means that you're living by the right rules already. It means you're starting off motherhood modelling the right stuff. Which means you're already on the path to raising that strong, independent kid you were fixing to raise. You're starting to raise a feminist. Bonus!

> *It's absolutely not what I thought it was going to be. I thought, in typical Dawn-style, that I'd be able to organise her into my life, but we've all been organised into hers.*
>
> Dawn French, on having a daughter

Call your own shots: make your own rules!

Remember, you don't have to be . . .

♦ Dressed

♦ Clean

♦ Sociable

♦ Fitting back into your jeans by Friday

♦ Shagging by Sunday (or, for that matter, dutifully abstaining from shagging for the next six weeks . . .)*

*If you fear for your lady parts, given their recent adventures, get them looked at by someone clinical before diving back in. After all, it feels like *EVERYONE* has had a look recently, eh? Feel HEALED first, love.

And you don't have to feel:

♦ Blissed out

♦ Thrilled

♦ In love with your baby straight away

♦ Different

YOU DON'T HAVE TO BREASTFEED!

Pregnancy, childbirth, sleepless nights, sore nipples and 3 a.m. feeds . . . Exhausting, huh? Music time. Hit Captain & Tenille's 'Do That To Me One More Time'. You might feel better if you sing along through gritted teeth, in the style of EastEnders' Phil Mitchell.

Chapter 4

'Put Your Coat On, You're About to Feel Cold'
Raising kids with choices

Al

It's February. There's snow on the ground. My children are little – maybe two and four. We've been indoors all day and I'm stir crazy: time for air, coffee and company. It's below zero outside. My son has had a snotty nose since about October; he's going to need a coat. This is a problem.

My daughter's been standing in the hallway of our house, fully bundled up for maybe a quarter of an hour already. She's red-faced as she strokes the pom-poms on the end of her scarf with thickly gloved hands that have turned each finger into a different Disney princess. By contrast, my son has reluctantly agreed to keep his sweater and trousers on, but is resolutely refusing to even *look* at his coat, let alone his woolly hat, which he has fed to the dog in what I'm choosing to interpret as gleeful defiance.

'But it's cold outside. Brrrrrrrr . . .' I venture, hoping my mimed shiver is an adequate demonstration of the validity of my logic. It isn't. Tom stands with his face twisted resolutely away from me and, significantly, also away from the coat, which I'm dancing in front of him. He's having none of it. Impasse.

I'm fifteen minutes into throwing the best I've got at this one: slapstick, sing-a-long, bribery and, as a last resort, reason. All I have left is a heap of unapologetic, arsy insistence. Besides anything else, I'm starting to wilt: I'm modelling the wrapped-up-warm state in which I would like my son to be and the stand-off is taking place right next to a radiator on full force. Plus, I'm squatting to get eye contact with my *refusenik*, and it's making my knees sweat.

And it doesn't dawn on me for a single moment. There I am, asserting the benefit of my experience over my little lad: *you are about to feel cold*, I'm telling him. *Trust me, I'm your mother. I know this about you.* Except that right in the glorious present of that moment, which is after all still his entire world at this point, my son *isn't* cold. In fact, he's overly warm, if anything. Why on *earth* would he want to put on a coat already?

I'm the one getting the situation wrong: all I see is defiance. He, quite rightly, sees a curious lack of logic on my part. He throws me a perplexed glance and then screws his eyes tight against the offending coat. Finally, all I see is red and I assert myself.

Moments later, we leave, all three of us wearing our coats. All three of us uncomfortably warm, two of us unhappy. (The third still blissfully lost in the finger-filled fairytale of her princess gloves.) Later, kids in bed, bra off, PJs and wine on, I finally see it: I had my own agenda to push, fuelled by a large dose of cabin fever. My 4-year-old son, by contrast, had been more than happy to comply with my key request. He was as keen to leave the house as I was, he just didn't yet feel the need for a coat. And so he stood his ground, confused by illogical adulthood, frustrated by the loss of control and upset about the removal of his right to make a choice that, after all, affected no one but him.

I could have played that scene out differently. I could have respected his choice, bided my time; headed out, coat on standby, and let the weather do its work. Moments would have passed. *Now I'm cold. Cold's not nice. I'd quite like that coat, now, Mum. And tomorrow, or the next day, I might remember this. And when I do, I might start using my coat as a preventative measure. Just like you do.*

I may have passed my insistence off as 'parenting', but for my lad, on the receiving end, it must have looked a lot like fascism. And if I wasn't showing him respect in the small things, how could I ask as much of him? How could I expect him to respect his sister's desire not to be trapped under an upturned laundry basket upon which he sits aloft for the entire duration of *Toy Story* until Dad finally hears her muffled cries? How could I ask that he respect the ever-patient dog's desire not to be locked out in the rain, dressed in swimming trunks, rubber ring and goggles? Or hope that he respects his mum and dad's desire not to have a full drum kit hauled in its entirety onto their bed at 5 a.m. on a Saturday morning for a twenty-minute demo? Because the real problem with my approach was that if I wasn't making damn sure my son knew how it feels to have someone respect your choices, even when you're only four (*especially* when you're only four), how could I expect him to grow up to respect the choices of others?

Unlike us grown-ups, toddlers, I am convinced, instinctively know this; they get it. They see that respect is like spaghetti: you have to throw plenty of it their way for it to have any real hope of sticking.

> *Children are remarkable for their intelligence and ardor, for their curiosity, their intolerance of shams, the clarity and ruthlessness of their vision.*
>
> Aldous Huxley, Complete Essays 3, 1930–1935

SO...

How to teach a concept so intangible as personal space to your young children? Seems like a big ask, no? The fact is, no amount of discussion about personal space with your 6-year-old is going to mean much, far more effective to *live it*. Weave it into the fabric of your parenting. Respect your kids' personal space and then talk to them about what that means.

Inevitably there are times when we have to go ahead and invade that space with younger children, even when they don't like it – plenty of times (to dole out drops for sticky eye, for instance). But all the more reason, then, that we know when to let the small stuff go. So pick your battles: manners, health and hygiene matter, matching Moschino baby not so much.

The flip side of teaching kids about respecting the personal space of others is to make absolutely sure they get to experience their *own* personal space. That means we need to weave real choices into their lives and an emerging sense of control over the way things roll – often; daily, actually. So let's just focus on three of the biggest routines of life at home with a young child.

♦ Getting dressed: Most of the time, so long as they are clean and warm and dry, what they choose to wear is their shout. If your 6-year-old rocks up at Nan's kitted up like a small, slightly camp despot, let it go; Nan can handle it. A friend's daughter once selected black wellies, fake armour, neon pearls and a Dolly Parton wig – for church. Why pitch yourself against choices that bold? Stick to practicalities: if it's cold outside, carry extra layers and wait until you can see they feel it. Then wearing that coat shouldn't be such an issue. Hand over a little control; it's tough being a wee 'un in an adult world.

♦ Getting clean: Lots of kids loathe their hair being brushed or their teeth being cleaned. That stuff is up close and personal and besides, for some it comes with a whole host of sensations bordering on intolerable (Carol Stock Kranowitz's *The Out-of-Sync Child* is quite brilliant on this). So put them in the driving seat. Show them how to do it, or get older brothers, sisters or cousins to show them how to do it. Take time over it, lose the tension; take the 'instruction' out of your voice. Kit yourself up: get a stash of that nicely scented detangle stuff for their hair and an attractive whizzy toothbrush of their choice and then let them get on with it.

♦ Show, don't tell: it works wonders.

And remember to big them up for a job well done (even if at first it's carnage in the bathroom and their hair still looks like something that just rocked up at Battersea Dogs & Cats Home). Small steps . . . They'll get there.

♦ Getting fed: While we're on the subject of choice, if she refuses to eat her peas and he chucks his broccoli at the dog, don't sweat it. Seriously, chill. *Your* job as a parent is to make sure that over the course of every week, you're plating up a wide range of good food for your kids. Variety on a plate, that's it. *Their job* is to decide what they want to eat — if anything — from each meal. Trust us, there's science behind this. You get to control *what* is put in front of them and *where* they are allowed to eat. But that's it: you don't get to control *how much* of that food gets into their stomachs at any one sitting.

Do not be tempted to turn the dinner table into a battleground — that way lies years of misery, for all of you.

Studies have shown that where parents serve up a good balanced diet but then adopt a stress-free, personal choice approach to mealtimes, kids invariably *choose* a good balance of foods over the course of a week. And kids who are handed this control over the amount of food they eat in one sitting invariably develop healthy habits of eating when they're hungry and stopping when they're full. Check out Jill Castle and Maryann Jacobsen's *Fearless Feeding: How to Raise Healthy Eaters From High Chair to High School*.

So, eat alongside them, chat, laugh and trust them to listen to their own bodies. Keep the spotlight off the kids at the table, in the wardrobe and in the bathroom. Bite your lip, respect their personal space and keep your sights firmly set on enabling them to develop a strong self-esteem and an emerging sense of themselves as independent young human beings with real control over their world and genuine choice in their daily lives.

Loosen those reins and let them taste how it feels to call some of their own shots. Immerse them in the give-and-take of human interaction. Honestly, these are *huge* lessons you're teaching them – about what's an acceptable degree of interference in our relationships with others, and what's not.

Don't just talk about it, live it; show, don't tell.

> *Children are educated by what the grown-up is and not by his talk.*
>
> *Carl Jung*, The Archetypes and the Collective Unconscious

Macklemore's glorious ode to his newborn daughter, 'Growing Up (Sloane's Song)', recorded with Ryan Lewis and Ed Sheeran, is a 'Mockingbird' song for the twenty-first century. None of your pointless promises about diamond rings and caged birds, this is all heart. More to the point, it perfectly sums up the 'Good Enough' school of parenting we need to tap into and dishes out life advice that's not about always colouring inside the lines. This guy knows it; he knows that kids are always going to take risks. He knows that we can't fix everything, so we need to quit trying. Give it a listen: the man talks sense.

Chapter 5

Mates, Allies and Co-conspirators: Finding Your Tribe Among the Other Mothers

Raising relaxed kids and parents

Vik

My sister is the most authentic person on the planet. This is annoying. In my early nineties' bid towards a middle-class family life – friends with degrees, tribal art, couscous – I would despair of her as she meandered her way with quiet assurance, like our mother before us, through raising our first-borns side by side. She would rather read *Heat Magazine* than any kind of parenting manual.

'Oh Christ, boring!' she'd say and wipe a passing nose. Occasionally, it was attached to a small child.

I thought she was a bit lazy and would make erroneous name-tape choices that would affect her children's long-term potential. I would read child psychology books and quote them, smugly, to her and my mother over the top of *Knot's Landing* or *Murder She Wrote*. I was *ON* it, me!

So it came to our boys starting school. We made the little blokes dap-bags for their PE kits. I made a mental note to search out the women I would consider 'like-minded' and quickly befriend them. When, on Day Two, I saw one wearing tie-dye and carrying the *Guardian*, I nearly peed, I was so thrilled: 'She's mine!'

Soon, the boys came home with their reading folders. The contents of these innocuous-looking receptacles were incendiary: suburban parental IEDs. Where your child was in the reading scheme was *EVERYTHING*. Me, not working at the time, I would congregate with other mothers in the playground around 9.13 a.m. and discuss this with a mixture of anxiety and injustice. Or, if it was our own kid on 'Yellow Hat 4', a tilty-head look of faux concern for their failing sprog laced with unadulterated 'Screw you, hun! My kid is a pigging *genius*!'

Meanwhile my sister was about as interested in being immersed with these mothers as she was about scuba diving. She cared hugely about her boys' education but would hang on the edges of the conversations, nodding and smiling every now and again, impatient for me to finish my self-congratulatory diatribe about Jean Piaget (I was doing an OU education course and knew *everything*). We would then walk home with our babies and the talk would turn to laundry and soap operas.

On one particular day I was expressing my concern about my son and his maths progress and she yawned . . . *in my face*. I said tersely, 'Don't you worry about all of this?' and she replied, 'Not really. Maybe I should but they seem happy, the boys, right? I miss H like mad now he's at school so when he gets home I just want to slob out with him, like it was before, watch a bit of *Brum* and eat crap. Those women up there, bloody hell – school is all they talk about! They all look the same, dress the same – who *ARE* they really? And I bet half their husbands are shagging someone at work cause they're so *dull*. You get too involved with it all, love.'

It was one of those crystal moments that always came courtesy of one of the women in my family. Buried within a hilarious, highly judgemental (and possibly slanderous) take on the immediate sisterhood, she made a lot of sense. It's the trap we fall into in the primary years; being academically neurotic, losing sight of the balance kids need between work and play, and crucially, our identity as women being submerged into our role as mothers. What would my boy, and my daughter, four years behind him, see in the way I navigated those years for them, and for me?

She wasn't all great calls, mind, my sister – the unlikely oracle. On the first parents' evening, she arrived just after us and sought me out. We nattered and then I noticed the legend emblazoned on her T-shirt, which was just visible under her cardi. I looked at her and nodded towards it. She glanced down and said, 'Shit! They are *never* going to take me seriously here, are they?' It said: *'Porn Star in Training'*.

'No, love,' I replied.

By now there was already a hot feeling of peer pressure in the playground – on me, not my boy (he was tickety-boo). I needed to step back, ease up and get to know some of these women. Possibly not the one with the *Observer Food Monthly* and the hand-crocheted leggings (we would have to see). I quite liked the look of the one with *Heat Magazine*, mind.

> *H: I feel I could have achieved more for them. I could have*
>   *been a doctor.*
> *Me: Are they doctors?*
> *H: No, but they're bi-lingual and love opera.*
> *Me: Well, you speak Greek and you're vegetarian by*
>   *choice.*
> *H: I suppose.*
>
> Nina Stibbe, Love, Nina: Despatches From Family Life

SO . . .

♦ Most other mums and dads are just as anxious as you are. Smile, have a chat – it's only a few minutes of your life each day. Your child will watch you and see that getting along with lots of different types of people is cool and relatively easy with minimal effort. Chat about stuff that isn't schoolwork and kids' progress.

♦ Don't dress up to take your child to school in the morning. Laugh at the very *idea* of having to be immaculate and clad in Jigsaw at 8.15 a.m. Focus on everyone being (mostly) clean, fed and on time. Turn up the radio and dance along to Usher, like a small act – 'The Von Tramps' (if you've badly misjudged laundry again). Your kids will love you for this. They won't feel under pressure to be perfect because clearly, you're not. Spit spot!

♦ Don't get academically neurotic. We know, it's hard – and we've done it, so we get the traps. Love and listen to your child, surround him/her with fun and stimulating experiences and people if you can, but don't start to die inside if s/he appears not to have the hallmarks of a future cardiothoracic surgeon when in Year 2. They will learn at their pace and find what lights them up. Fossils, footie, fractions . . . time will tell. They need to know that *their* homework is not *your* life – or theirs. Talk to other mums about taking this approach; they will probably feel deeply grateful. We can give each other permission or judgement – you decide what feels best.

♦ You are going to find some other parents you do actually quite like. Try the friendship on for size, as you would any other. If it gets intense or they turn out to be a spelling-test bore, ease back with grace and kindness and don't feel bad about it. If your kids are best buddies, there's no reason for that to stop. But chances are, there will be someone you can knock back the bourbon with and slag off David Cameron. Marvellous! Sisterhood at its best. Your kids seeing this: priceless.

♦ Remember who the grown-ups are. Try not to get overly involved in the rise and fall of kids' friendships. They will change and you just need to wait in the wings, watch from a distance and provide a safe haven when it's painful. You can't protect them from this; it's necessary stuff. Even when you want to bludgeon that little shit Bradley to death for leaving your baby off the party list.

♦ Don't feel obliged to get involved in the PTA or hearing readers. If you are working and just can't fit that kinda stuff in, fine. Some folk love it and have time so let them get on with it. Don't feel guilty, even when some (other mothers, chances are) try to make you. You've got your world and if you get a Tuesday morning to yourself and you choose to spend it watching *House of Cards* rather than wearing a day-glo vest and supporting cycling proficiency, cracking, do that! If you love being around littlies and organising stuff, power to you! Flatter those mums madly. Chances are they need it more than you do. Getting a girls' footie team going though? YES!

♦ Let the kids see you being both interested in them, and interested in the world outside of them. Mum, maker of muffins, ain't the whole picture. Mum, maker of movies or Excel spreadsheets, now that's more like it! Mum saying the F-word at that nice Mr Boris who lives with the Queen when he comes on telly, even better. (I realise this is advocating swearing in front of children but that's very middle class — I still can't help myself.)

♦ Have as many kids over to your place as often as you can. You don't have to spend a lot of money and for Christ's sake, don't get pulled into party guilt! In summer, hose kids down until they practically drown in larfs and snot and then in winter, do a full-on soup 'n cheap rolls picnic in the park. Kids mostly just want to be around other kids; they want the chance to step out of the hothouse of school and form bonds with each other in the safety of their home environments. Mix up the genders. Give not a damn about how tidy your place is, make it a fun palace of music and laughter for small folk when your time and energy allows. Don't ask them about their SATS or grades. Ever. If you've gone with non-judgement of other mums, ask one or two of them to hang out and have a gin at the end. Or get a sitter and fall down the pub. Give one another the green flag to lighten up and offload as often as you can. And then when they're teenagers, the other kids will keep coming back. In fact, you can't get rid of the buggers (maybe this is crap advice!).

♦ Parents aren't only connected through having a sweaty, glorious 4-year-old. We're united by so much more than having kids. We are all stood there, in February, shivering and internally churning around and kicking ourselves to death over work and money and sex and guilt and weight/hairlines and austerity measures (or versions of that list). It's just with some (no, most) of us, because we're human and flawed that then often translates into insecurity, comparison and competition. You don't have to be friends with everyone, but starting with empathy and openness is much more likely to lead to some fun and maybe even supportive connections. You want your child to get stuck in and take risks socially, why not do the same? Roll up, role model!

♦ Relish these years. Seriously. You will miss your children when they're gone because once they go into Year 7 and beyond, the sense of community that happens around primary schools goes. *BIG* opportunity in these seven years to send highly enabling messages about all the qualities of good feminism: being nice and fair to each other, being authentic and having a cracking good time before you change the world . . . after tea!

We could do a lot worse than to take a lead from David Bowie on this one: listen really carefully to his fabulous 'Kooks'. Then put away their maths homework and start the car.

Chapter 6

A Thousand Paths: The Importance of Space in Childhood
Raising self-motivated kids

Al

In the mid-1990s, I spent three years teaching history in a highly academic London girls' school. There were roughly a thousand girls on the roll and academically, the place *buzzed*. The girls were generally hungry to learn, devouring the history of the American West, the Arab-Israeli Conflict, Ireland . . . Discovering for the first time that injustice and subjugation form the backbone of recorded history, they were keen to understand the context which enabled that injustice, fired up by the courage and foresight of those who rallied against the system. It was a *fabulous* place to teach.

It was also my first experience of a truly multi-cultural school and of an exclusively female student body and it would hugely inform the parent, and the feminist, I was about to become. As I helped my students come to a more informed opinion about the injustices of the past, they quietly helped me take a good, hard look at some of my own opinions.

Initially, the challenge for me was to get my thoughts straight about the families who already had their daughters' futures very much mapped out. I'm referring to those girls whose futures were dictated specifically by their cultural and religious inheritances. There were marriages already on the horizon for some, for instance: future marriages being discussed on behalf of 15-year-old girls. Then there were other girls working tirelessly at their studies despite knowing that the religious community in which they were being raised forbade them from taking up careers. (Yes, *forbade* this.)

It was a revelation to me, the degree to which I was unsettled that the lives of these brilliant, vibrant, beautiful young girls would take such an unrecognisable path from my own. Much of my time there was spent feeling enraged on their behalf. I felt keenly what a loss to the world the limitations placed on their futures would represent. But the experience of teaching a shining soul named Mariella changed my perception entirely.

Mariella was from a non-denominational, white, wealthy North London family. She had a brilliant mind and a kind heart and was devoted to her studies. Beautiful and effortlessly successful in everything she turned her hand and mind to, she was widely adored by the other girls. Here was a capable and generous leader in the making. And yet, as it turned out, she was relentlessly incapable of convincing her mother of any of this.

I began teaching her when she was fourteen, by which time her schedule was intimidating: daily two- or three-hour training sessions in the pool, gym and tennis courts. In addition, there were sessions of tuition throughout the week in elocution, Latin, piano and oboe, and a yoga session every morning in her own home with her mother and a visiting instructor. Her day started eye-wateringly early and she said invariably it was 8 p.m. before she could sit down to her studies, and often later.

In the run-up to GCSEs, she was visibly buckling. I asked why she didn't think about thinning down her extra-curricular activities a little. She looked up at me from her seat, her eyes filling with tears, and said nothing. And I scolded myself for not having realised before: *none* of this was of her own choosing. Her mother's choices dictated her daughter's every waking moment. Mariella was nothing but a ball girl on the tennis court of her own life. Quitting wasn't an option and so I said the only thing I could: 'I'm so sorry.'

Parents' Evening set everything into stark relief for me. Pretti's Hindi family turned up en masse. I was nervous, aware that they were embarking on the business of finding their young daughter a future husband and consequently, not at all sure how I would handle a face-to-face. Around the table gathered mother, daughter, sister, big brother and father. They were a warm and friendly team, constantly talking all at once and falling about laughing each time they did so. *Was Pretti working too hard?* they wanted to know. (I agreed – she was a powerhouse and could well afford to ease off a little.) *Had she gained in confidence?* asked Mum. ('Without doubt,' I said.) *Was she more often speaking out in class now?* her big brother asked. ('Yes, all the time,' I told them.) *Was she gutsier in putting her arguments across?* Dad wanted to know. ('Gutsy?' I said. 'She's *FEARLESS*!')

The family oozed love and care and respect. They didn't need to ask if she was dedicated, conscientious; already they knew and trusted this about her. And they cared palpably about every aspect of Pretti's development. All five of them fizzed with pride at her successes. As they stood to leave, her big brother swept Pretti up and congratulated his sister while Mum and Dad beamed at each other. They were not at all what I had anticipated – they were *fabulous*!

Reagan's family were part of the Brethren community and as such, she would be steered just as resolutely towards marriage and motherhood as would Pretti. But there would be no room in Reagan's future for ambition, no question of her pursuing a career, or even working for a living. That just wasn't how her community rolled. Hers was an alien world to me, and I was deeply curious to meet her family.

In the event, Reagan's family were no less awesome than Pretti's, their family bond no less palpable. They were every bit the quiet, respectful, centred people I had expected, given that those traits characterised the vast majority of the Brethren girls in my classes. But for all their demure ways, they were far from joyless: Reagan and her mother giggled into each other's shoulders like sisters when her father mispronounced my name, and when I stopped blethering long enough to listen, her mother had a wry sense of humour that was just *brilliant*.

And then, Reagan gave voice to how she felt she had performed so far that year; she spoke straightforwardly, honestly and without ego. She gave herself credit where it was due and correctly pinpointed a couple of areas in which she felt she could improve. Then she thanked me for a couple of aspects of the lessons she had found useful and named a few friends she had found helpful study partners: generous, honest, lovely. And the undisguised adulation in her parents' eyes as they listened to her made my own eyes well up.

There was love and respect and peace bedded down at the heart of this family – it was a beautiful, tangible thing. Reagan was being raised within a close-knit community with its own idiosyncratic take on life, but she was *no* victim. Here was a nurtured and valued *individual*, undeniably secure in the love and respect with which she was surrounded. Seeing her in that context, I was in awe of the grounded, inspirational and utterly secure woman she was fast turning into.

None of this was as I had anticipated.

And then Mariella came to the table with her mother: her blonde, manicured, trim, toned, beautiful mother, dressed in tennis whites, glancing constantly down at her expensive watch with thinly veiled irritation. Next to her sat Mariella, occupying as tiny a space as she could, her limbs folded in on herself, eyes down, colour drained. Neither made eye contact, both painstakingly avoiding physical contact with the other. The tension was like nothing I'd experienced before. *Was this her life?*

I set out in praise of everything Mariella – not difficult, she was a remarkable girl. But the more I talked up her dedication and ability and potential, the more I realised her mother was leaking a tight-lipped scepticism. She was sighing, restlessly shifting her weight away from me in her chair and at one point, tutted. It was utterly counter-intuitive and it threw me; within moments, I was stammering, losing my train of thought, doubting myself: she had *frightened* me.

Once I'd finished, she started, effectively tearing into everything I said. She didn't doubt her daughter was managing to *appear* a polite, hard-working, conscientious type, but she warned me (*WARNED* me) not to be fooled: this was categorically *not* the 'real' Mariella. She talked about her remotely, as if Mariella wasn't actually sat by her side, but was elsewhere. Mariella looked broken, vacant; elsewhere, in fact.

I was bewildered.

For sure, doors were closed to some of these girls from the off by the communities, faiths and cultural inheritances into which they were born. In that respect, their belief systems were, in part, alien to me. But Reagan, Pretti and their like were bright, happy, secure and *lovely* young women, driven to learn and to discover the full reach of their potential and emerging from the quagmire of adolescence largely intact. Far from raging against the machine of their upbringing, they were poised on the brink of a future that they appeared to be wholly embracing.

In contrast, Mariella ostensibly had the wealth of choice, freedom and potential I wanted for all the girls, and yet she was being stifled by a chilling lack of trust, empathy and respect from the one person whose assurances she needed most. And of the three of them, it was Mariella who was the most imprisoned. The thought of what her future held worried me far, far more.

Pretti, Reagan and Mariella triumphed in their GCSEs, and all signed up for A-level history, but by the time Mariella came back to the sixth form in the autumn, the decline which had set in before the summer exams had taken full hold. She had grown worryingly thin, her skin grey and spotted and covered in a fine down, the shine gone from her, physically and metaphorically. She wore a thin and unconvincing smile, averted her gaze and barely spoke. When she did, it was never a full sentence. Quietly in the background, the wheels of support were set into motion by senior teachers and I was devastated for her.

Four weeks into term, she came to let me know she was dropping out. More than that, she was *moving* out. She was moving in with her 28-year-old boyfriend and had a plan: a market stall selling old vinyl and CDs. It was what she wanted, she said – her own path, her own pace, her own rules.

She had been one of the brightest students I had encountered and was throwing it away for (as it turned out), a doped-up, inked-up fella who had been busy flunking his GCSEs when she was still just four years old. I was heartbroken for her, but I got it: *he* was her choice and she was very, very new to the business of making choices.

I'd seen a thousand different versions of girlhood at the school, a thousand different paths to emerging womanhood. Who was I to judge?

By the end of that academic year, I was pregnant with my first child. Over my three years at the girls' school I'd seen enough to feel more than a little trepidation about the kind of parent I would turn out to be. Naturally I was excited and already had a head full of dreams, but late at night, the fact that I was already dreaming on behalf of my baby troubled me. I wanted to enjoy, enable, enrich and equip my child, but most of all, I wanted to shut up long enough to listen and stand back far enough to let my kids find their own path.

SO . . .

We're all working for the same thing: robust, self-reliant, creative, empathetic kids. Kids who grow up to know who they are, what they want and are prepared to work hard to get there; kids who can handle setbacks, disappointment, failure. There's nothing wrong with that as a set of goals, it's the backbone of what any one of us needs to feel grounded, confident, capable. And yes, it strikes at the heart of what feminist parenting should be all about. The problem is that somehow the Extra-Curricular Club seems to have become our main *mode d'emploi*. Because let's be honest, we *fill* our kids' lives. We all know this about ourselves. We choreograph their leisure time with sports clubs, swimming lessons, ballet, music, drama . . . We're working from the right place in all of this: we do it because we want them to be emotionally and physically robust team players. We want to help them explore a bunch of creative stuff until they find their 'thing', their path to self-expression.

But it can get out of hand. Our generation want daughters who are as fearless on the rugby pitch as they are flexible at the ballet barre. We want sons who throw themselves as heartily into the camaraderie of the changing rooms as they do a music, art, dance or drama studio. We want it all. And none of this stuff is inherently bad. It's not bad that we queue for our kids' swimming lessons, or ferry them from rugby to ballet to piano to Scouts to drama. Or even that we gently nag them to practise their violin. But it *is* bad that somewhere along the line, we have forgotten what our parents' generation seemed to know instinctively: we can't *impose* these qualities on our kids. No amount of subs paid, places booked or certificates blu-tacked to the fridge will guarantee that any of this gets properly bedded down.

We figured this stuff out, eventually; we felt our way through it. Bit by bit we learned it via a series of long, unsupervised adventures: with our siblings and a sea of imaginary crocodiles on the upstairs landing on rainy days. With the neighbours' kids on sunny days, Chopper bikes at dawn and a full set of bloody knees by dusk; with a playground full of British Bulldogs. Alone all day with our noses buried in C. S. Lewis, or glued to the terrors of *Dr Who* and the exquisite agony of *White Horses*. Thanks to the genius of the benignly neglectful school of parenting, we had the glorious luxury of childhoods lit by time and space.

It is so important that we fight the urge to micromanage that same space and freedom out of our kids' lives. Time we stopped seeing a kid with time on its hands as a thing to be feared. Time to put back those chinks of time and space. Space in early childhood to discover what boredom feels like, and then a bit more time to figure out what to do about it; space in adolescence to lie around for hours, listening to mournful music and replaying the trials and tribulations of the week until a path through the lunacy starts to reveal itself. And the space to try out a few versions of themselves until they find one that feels comfy.

On reflection, then, our role in all of this is actually very simple:

♦ Lead the way: we teach by example, not by word, so as often as you can, model the things you want them to learn – energy, hard work, fun, persistence, optimism. An ability to find the fun in every situation, to pick yourself up after setbacks, to *relish* an empty hour. And keep going; they won't see it immediately but they will, in time.

♦ Step back: listen to them. Listen to what they're telling you with their words and also with their actions. Let them take the reins more; let them steer a path through their own free time. Make suggestions, where you feel the need, but don't dictate.

♦ Watch, praise, enjoy: they are a different animal from you. They won't make the same choices, or the same mistakes – they'll make a new set, all of their own. So stop working out of anxiety; trust them. They're fabulous, they'll figure it out – and they'll be so much more brilliant at it than you ever expected.

> *Most women are resourceful: when faced with boredom, they find a way out. That's an essential skill. Those who don't have it will suffer, to be sure.*
>
> Suzanne Venker, The Flipside of Feminism

Point is, it's all about the journey – that luscious, lovely, unpredictable journey that leads our kids to wherever they're headed. We want so badly to teach our kids what we've learned about life all at once. But hey, that's not the way. Natasha Bedingfield's 'Freckles' says it all beautifully. They'll get there – it will all be OK.

Chapter 7

Finding the Fabulousness and Staying in the Arena
Raising optimistic kids

Al

I'm not naturally an enormously optimistic person, but I'm learning
. . . Every Thursday morning for eighteen months while my son was
still too young for school, Mary would erupt into my little home,
brimming with sunshine and drenched in soft pinks, perfume and
pearls. Mary was my son's physiotherapist. My kids – still only
eighteen months and three years old when Mary first came into our
lives – adored her.

I loved her too. She filled every space and lit up every dark corner; she
was utterly contagious. Like some cosy housemistress from a home
counties boarding school for girls, she combined poise and authority
with affection and optimism in perfect measure, sufficient to reassure
me that I could exhale for an hour a week, safe, in her company.

I loved her, too, for her *certainty* that my son's future was going to be
fabulous. With every puzzle piece he slotted into place, every animal

noise he attempted to make, her unfettered delight convinced me that she had marked my boy out as exceptional. At frequent intervals, her default setting of remarkable joy would buckle under the weight of love for her work, and she would give in to a moment of euphoria. She would suddenly throw off whatever piece of kit with which she was delighting my son and help herself to large dollops of him, nuzzling her face into his and declaring, bewilderingly, 'Ooh, you're a *sinner!*' – exuberance my little boy would match, ounce for ounce.

She was married to an imposing and wealthy farmer and they had put down roots in a farmhouse so vast she was once entirely thrown when I asked her how many bedrooms there were; in more than thirty years, she had never thought to count. For all that, though, theirs was a working farm: neither were strangers to graft. During lambing season, Mary would often appear at the door as fresh and groomed as ever in her soft pink cloud, but traces of mud beneath her fingernails evidenced that her day began hours before daylight, helping her husband bring new life into the world.

Her own kids were grown and flown, but had all been blessed with super-size helpings of their mother's fabulousness. She had instilled in each of them an absolute belief that they were *enough*: that there was nothing fate could throw at them that a love of life and unstinting hard work wouldn't turn into something altogether wonderful.

They appeared to be living lives that stood testament to that philosophy. Her daughter, for instance, grappled with a not insignificant dyslexia before the British education system was fully ready to acknowledge the condition. Undeterred, Mary's daughter set her sights on a career in journalism, and fought a series of remarkable battles with enormous self-belief and charisma until she got to where she wanted to be. Buoyed by her mother's rosy-hued cloudburst, how could she not have soared?

One Thursday, Mary turned up at our door, eyes twinkling characteristically from behind an enormous box filled with magical bits of kit. But as she settled herself on the lounge floor, I felt none of her usual bounce. She was as captivating and brilliant as ever during the session, but nonetheless, something was missing: she moved less than usual, sparkled a little less.

Over a cuppa afterwards, I hesitated. I could see all wasn't well, but felt awkward about asking her. She brought endless joy to our lives on a weekly basis and in return, I thanked her copiously, made her tea in her favourite mug (she even enthused about my crockery) and attempted, often, to tell her what an enormous difference she was making. But I wasn't her *friend* – this was work for her, after all – and I didn't know how to embark upon crossing what I perceived to be a line.

As it happened, she spoke first.

'I'm afraid I'm not going to see you for a few weeks. I'm going in for surgery.' And for the first time, an unchecked, unmistakable flicker of anxiety crossed her face. But before I could say anything at all, she threw it off again, with reassurances about how fabulously my boy was coming on, with words of praise and encouragement for me and with an entire toy kit, with which we were to keep ourselves busy in her absence. Then, scooping up Tom for one last greedy nuzzle, she was gone.

It was only later that I learned that Mary's surgery was to treat a long-standing, debilitating and painful condition with which she must have been battling for a very long time. In all the time we had known her, in fact, she could rarely have been pain-free. I was staggered, as much by my own apparent lack of empathy as by her predicament. How could I have missed it? How could I have been so self-absorbed? Except I hadn't missed it: the truth was, she hadn't revealed it, not a glimpse of it, until that last morning with us before her surgery. In all the time she had spent with us, and with anyone else, as it turned out, she resolutely refused to let pain define her and had instead tapped into her remarkable, unchecked love of life, holding a mirror up to the very best in every person she met along the way.

Naturally, Mary's irrepressible spirit wasn't about to be contained by any surgery or NHS pain management plan and in no time at all, she was back, filling our home and our hearts as much as ever before. Sixteen years have elapsed since then and she's still working, promoted now to lead a team. I have no doubt that she lights up every one of her team, effortlessly introducing them all to the best in themselves.

Her children, too, have continued to soar. They don't appear ever to have lost that sheer delight in everything the world has to offer. It's not money or privilege that made them that way, it's their mother's relentless empathy, her ability to tap into the glorious potential and beauty of every spirit she encounters. Because as it turns out, seeing the fabulousness of others *is* contagious but it's nothing you can teach – you have to live it, feel it and give in to the loveliness of it, whenever you encounter it. And it's enormously invigorating.

I think of Mary often, particularly when something delights me. I've discovered that there's an energy that comes from giving in to the *fabulousness* of others in the way Mary continuously modelled. I think that may just have been her secret. She instinctively rode the wave of euphoria wherever she felt it, letting it wash away the anxious flotsam of daily life. Search for the loveliness of the moment and you're automatically rooting yourself in the 'now'.

Surely that must be at the root of any family ethos, not least a feminist one. The belief that people are endlessly fascinating; that folk respond best when you help them to see how *fabulous* they are, how *fabulous* they will become, regardless of gender, race or disability. Holding a mirror up to the best in people and then *delighting* in what they then reveal themselves capable of. That *has* to be at the heart of management, teaching, marriage – and parenting.

I try really hard to live by it, though it's by no means the effortless instinct for me as it is for Mary. But I persevere, for my own sake, but mostly for my children's sakes. And just once in a while, when I sense the Black Dog lingering at the door, I cocoon myself in a little bit of pink, just to help the day along.

> *Optimism is the faith that leads to achievement. Nothing can be done without hope and confidence.*
>
> *Helen Keller*, Optimism

Feminism used to be angry. And for a while, I guess anger was what was needed. But sooner or later, anger grows wearisome. We neither want nor need to stay angry any more. What we need now is optimism. Keep saying what we want, keep working for what we want and, crucially, keep believing we'll get there. What better philosophy within which to raise kids? Optimism is the new anger.

I envy the lucky few who find optimism a natural state of being. I'm not one of their number but it's a muscle we can all flex.

SO . . .

♦ Catch yourself in the moment you're overwhelmed by a gloomy prediction of a miserable outcome. For a moment, force yourself to give voice to the polar opposite possibility – out loud!

♦ Concentrate really hard on doing this in front of the kids. Regardless of whether the conversation directly involves them or not, try to balance out the pessimist in you for their sake. Fake optimism is better than nothing, for now.

♦ *Always* give your kids a rosier alternative to any potential failure they predict in their own lives. But remember that no amount of this will help unless they hear you do the same with your own shit on a regular basis. Model it, live it, teach it.

♦ The American writer Dorothy Parker said she found, 'London is satisfied, Paris is resigned, but New York is always hopeful. Always it believes that something good is about to come off, and it must hurry to meet it.' Feminist parenting is inherently optimistic: we need to create a childhood filled with the belief that something fabulous and fascinating is imminently about to happen. We need to be more New York.

You know it makes sense. Find the fabulousness: it makes you feel great, it makes them feel great, it gives your kids their best shot at a life filled with unlocked potential. And it doesn't get any more fabulous than Aretha singing '(You Make Me Feel Like) A Natural Woman', preferably the time she belted it out to Carole King with the Obamas watching on at the 38th Annual Kennedy Center Honors.

Chapter 8

'Boys Don't Cry': Emotional Intelligence
Raising emotionally intelligent kids

Al

This feels as good a time as any to talk about Ash. Upfront, I ought perhaps to come clean: Ash's family wasn't a family I knew intimately. I knew a version of them; the one Ash felt the need to share. And I filled in *LOTS* of gaps all by myself. I should also add that there's not much by way of 'sisterhood' in what follows, but bear with me.

Ash was fifteen when he joined my tutor group at a North London comprehensive school. Bright-eyed and good-looking, he threw himself into life in his new school, and won the lead in the school play, Simon Stephens' *Herons*. As I was about to discover, the bruised and lonely Billy was perfect casting.

Ash soon palled up with a reserved but generous soul from the tutor group named Bronwyn. Bronty swam against the tide, and was all the more fascinating for it, but was yet to appear entirely comfortable steering that particular course. The two quickly became inseparable. They huddled on a deep window ledge outside my classroom each morning, curled up in each other; they spoke in whispers, shared myriad in-jokes and began to merge each other's sentences. At parents' evening close to half term, Bronty's mum told me Ash was spending so much time at their place, she was routinely cooking for five at weekends.

And yet, for all that, there was no hint of romance. Not even a whiff of any clumsy, exploratory teen stuff. Bronty adored Ash, that was evident, and he her, but this was quite obviously just friendship. I watched them lean into each other, emotionally; neither entirely comfortable in their own skin, each just a little out of step with their peer group; both bolstered by their new-found commonality. I was fascinated.

The first four months of their friendship proved to be the most challenging of Ash's life. It emerged that he had taken the enormously courageous decision to come out: first to Bronty, then to a couple of other friends, and then, one day after school in November, to me, buoyed by the ever-faithful Bronty at his side. At fifteen, this was no easy thing and the terror of rejection was painfully evident in his eyes. But there was no rejection: Bronty was effortlessly accepting, and I hugged him till I felt his shoulders relax and then asked if he wanted a Kit Kat.

After that, Ash began to open up more and more. He and Bronty would linger in my classroom over lunchtime or after school, chipping away at the stuff that was hooding his eyes with sadness and making his shoulders slump. His mother, he said, worked away in Oxford all week, sharing a house with a friend there and coming home at weekends to her husband and their two boys. Bronty said they'd only see Ash at her place on the weekends when his mother didn't come home. Lately, she said, they'd seen Ash pretty much every weekend.

Then, on the first morning back to school after the Christmas break, I found Ash and Bronty huddled together on their window ledge, conspiratorial, Ash's plaintive eyes peering over the top of a Christmas scarf; Bronty at his side, morose. Something was up. After registration, they lingered in the doorway.

Ash's Christmas, as it turned out, had been an exercise in humiliation. His extended paternal family was gargantuan and largely lived locally. Though he was still not out within his own family, everyone from his cousins to his father – even his nan – had made Ash the brunt of an endless line of crass jokes about effeminacy.

'They *loathe* queers,' he said, numbly. 'They see homophobia as a way to get a laugh – at my expense. They genuinely think it's funny. How do I come *out* to these people?' He sat, slumped into Bronty, holding her hand tightly.

'Bastards!' she said. And then, 'Come home with me, Friday'. *That word: home.*

Shit, I thought. He's *fifteen* and adrift. His absentee mother can't even begin to help him through any of this because she's not around long enough to find out anything about him. And he's submerged in a sea of old-school homophobia, with a well-meaning (and, God love him, an almost certainly cuckolded) father at the helm, who all appear to be entirely unaware that they're crushing the lad's spirit with every passing one-liner.

Bronty's mum later confided in me that Ash's mother hadn't come home at all for Christmas, nor for New Year. Ash spent New Year at Bronty's. Late on New Year's Day, Bronty's mum asked did he want her to run him home? Reluctantly, he called home. No response. He texted his older brother: he was away with mates. So he called his dad, who didn't pick up. Bronty's mum swung by the house: darkness.

It transpired that no one had asked him where he would be spending New Year. No one thought to find out when he'd be home. No one had even answered his calls.

It was 3 January before Ash went home that year, the night before term started. Four whole days and no one had thought to check.

I get it: marriages end, love affairs come crashing to a halt; people meet and fall in love. Really, I get it. And often, too, men and women reach a certain stage in their lives and realise that long ago they were wrong to have shelved their career/ambition/passion in exchange for a compromise in which they may once have believed whole-heartedly. Time passes, people change . . . we move on.

I've battled plenty of demons of my own, much of the time while simultaneously cooking fish fingers, planning birthday bashes or stitching nativity cow costumes. I'll admit too that I've had spells of having to fake it – going through the motions, working hard at parenting, getting by, trying to feel well. Telling them they're loved and lovely and all the while, battling against numbness. I've been there; we probably all have. It's depression and it's a bugger. But we *stay*. No matter what, we parent. Whether life interferes and forces us to live apart from our kids or whether we eat breakfast together every morning, we stay: we parent.

I can't know what was going on in that woman's life or head, and I'm not about to judge her or her marriage. But I will say one thing: Ash wasn't feeling like his mum was present in his life at that enormously crucial stage. Convinced his father was judging him, Ash felt his mother's absence all too keenly. *And Sister, that was a mistake. Swallow it up and start making amends.* When a kid feels judged, alone, labelled and lesser, us parents, we step up, no? That's the whole point of us, isn't it?

I have such an issue with labelling children. 'You're such a naughty boy/girl' instead of 'Slapping your nan was a naughty thing to do', or better yet, 'a poor choice'. Words, labels, they *matter*. Labels can be insidious. An old colleague of mine in leafy North London (who we secretly labelled 'Mrs Organic') routinely described the younger of her two girls as 'My Delicate One'. *From birth.* 'Poor Maggie,' she'd say, whenever there was a hiatus in conversation. She'd say it with affection but without any apparent good reason. (Maggie's health, as far as I could tell, was just as robust as her older sister's.) How *hard* would that kid have had to work to prove otherwise?

Similarly, the particulars of Ash's temperament, sensitivities, strengths and talents seemed to have been noted from the start. His family rightly spotted, for instance, his beautiful singing voice, his breath-taking artistry; his early capacity to root himself in a character onstage. No doubt they saw too that these were none of the things his brother had ever leaned towards. Consciously or not, the family steadily made their preferences clear to Ash. After fifteen years of it, he was in no doubt: his brother was the star. Team sports, science, sexist jokes, back-slapping and (in due course), lots of shagging. Ash, quiet, pretty, different: *lesser.*

Ash was always going to pick up on the subtleties of the family dynamic because let's face it, kids do. And so he continued to do what he loved, what he could do so effortlessly. But he also pushed himself to do everything else. Night after night he stayed up, sacrificing a good night's sleep for studying. He set his sights on brilliance and would be crushed by anything less.

As his sixteenth birthday passed, he also began to engineer regular encounters with drink, dope and dudes. Increasingly left to his own devices, he took more and more risks, pulled away from Bronty and the security of her family, struck out alone. He worried me to death; Bronty, bereft without him, worried me just as much.

Through it all, he studied hard. He got straight A*s and was briefly the talk of the school. At sixth form, he dropped the Arts, pushed himself towards science and maths and then pursued and won the ultimate accolade: Engineering at Oxbridge. Something his father would approve of; excellence in what was an indisputably male world.

I was delighted to see him succeed and made that clear to him. But I can't shake a sense of sadness for him, too – so much struggle . . .

I have agonised over this; I can *see* the differences between the two kids with an outsider's eye. Ash's drive, ambition and focus were quite remarkable in one so young, particularly given the hotbed of inadequacies from which they were born. And the end product was a level of academic excellence that, on paper, set him up for the brightest of futures. By comparison, at the age of sixteen, Bronty was yet to find Ash's strident self-reliance. Where he was crowd-surfing life's party, she was inching forward, hesitantly, in the queue for the bar.

Today, I see echoes of Bronty in my own daughter, who shows the same signs of strain as she refuses to buckle under the weight of peer convention. Their school careers, Bronty's and my daughter's, may not have had the razzamatazz of Ash's, and yet, like Bronty, my daughter has always known herself loved, lovely and needed. She knows we are in awe of her talents, of her gift for empathy. She knows too that a degree of failure is inevitable, but never insurmountable; that it's OK. And she knows we're always here.

I can't shake the injustice of Ash's path to self-discovery; he deserved a *fairer* upbringing, one in which he was valued for his creativity, his enormous emotional intelligence. He deserved that kind of security: he would still have shone, excelled, but he would have been working from a solid core.

To feel valued, nurtured. Equal. To be free to feel what you feel and explore your own talents . . . Isn't that what we all crave? It's *everything* our children need and it starts right at the beginning.

My own son arrived in this world with an almost ready-made emotional integrity that gave him a grounded confidence in himself. It didn't ever need a great deal of work. He also came with a significant learning disability that needed a very particular kind of nurturing – a time-consuming one – in order to equip him with the skills he needed to shine. My daughter: quick to learn, razor-sharp intellect and scrupulously moral, but a tentative over-thinker who continues to work hard to find some of her brother's confidence. They need, have always needed, very different things from their dad and me. We worked so hard to make sure neither looked upon their own particular place in the family as in any way *lesser*. Because equality, justice, fairness, it all starts there in your own home.

Ash was not *selfish* to make the choices he did when he pulled away from his family, though he once told me that was the label they pinned on him. He was simply adopting the model with which he had been raised: self-reliance. Similarly, he wasn't *lesser* for choosing to sing, act, paint and eschew rugby. Gesticulate a lot. Adopt a particular vocal pattern. Fall in love with men. He was just being himself.

I've discovered it's almost impossible to always get this stuff right, and that stuffing up from time to time is inevitable. But honesty, perseverance, love gets you by, so long as you're truly present in your kids' lives; emotionally present. No label was ever going to limit my children. Learning disability was never going to define my son; having a learning-disabled brother was never going to define my daughter. Just as she was *never* going to feel limited by the fact of her being a girl.

Labels: they're *insidious*.

I hope that being a fabulous, fascinating and endlessly creative young man, young gay man, has turned out to be nothing that Ash has come to see as limiting.

> *From Long Island to Silicon Valley, a fear of being perceived as weak forces men into pretending they are never afraid, lonely, confused, vulnerable, or wrong; and an extreme fear of being perceived as cold-hearted, imperfect, high-maintenance, or hostile forces women to pretend they're never exhausted, ambitious, pissed-off or even hungry.*
>
> Brené Brown, Rising Strong

SO . . .

There's so much here — so much that can feel enormously daunting, if you let it. In essence, however, there are two things worth remembering:

1. We all label our kids. Consciously or otherwise, we all hear that inner voice telling us, 'Ah, but this is *John*. Remember, tendency to play victim. He's probably exaggerating again', or 'Steady, tread softly here. Jane is terribly sensitive to failure. Let this one go . . .'

   So, take a moment, call it. Acknowledge now the things you think you know about your kids. And then try really, really hard to *stop* letting yourself be influenced by that — at least not all of the time. Catch yourself reacting to each of your kids: name it, quietly to yourself. And try harder to react differently the next time. That's all we can do: name it, acknowledge it, try harder.

2. Life isn't always the ride you'd hoped it would be — shit happens. Things can get really tough. And some days, steering a course through can take enormous effort. But if you're a parent, at some point in every day no matter what, you need to take the spotlight off yourself and shine it onto them. Go long, keep going; keep parenting. And take comfort in the fact that in spite of how tough a day it was,

you're still doing it. Shit passes; it'll all be all right. Meanwhile, you're doing great; your kids are great: you're enough.

> *No amount of money in the world can make up for parental absence. It's one of life's harshest realities.*
>
> Suzanne Venker, The Flipside of Feminism

We've all heard that theory that you can trick your brain into feeling better about itself using muscle memory. Fake a smile long enough and your brain thinks, 'Aha, OK! We're smiling. We must be feeling OK'. Music can do that too. Sing along to Pink's 'Fuckin' Perfect' and keep going till you believe her.

Chapter 9

Pink is Not a Crime: Navigating Gender Stereotypes With Your Daughter
Raising *your* daughter

Vik

I didn't get the Barbie memo.

My colleagues brought me quickly up to speed, though. Having packed my newly 5-year-old birthday girl off to school, I arrived, rushed but chipper, at the staff room, recalling how thrilled my girl was to unwrap her new hot-pink desk that morning.

'Oh God, not *Barbie*?' said the Head of Humanities, dunking her fourth Bourbon and looking aghast, as if I'd said, 'It was *such* a buzz seeing my baby's face opening her My Little Shotgun this morning! We all went, "Many Happy Returns darling, LOCK AND LOAD!"'

'I find it extraORDINARY that any parent would even consider buying one of those misogynistic pieces of plastic,' she went on.

'It's a desk. With pink bits on it,' I offered pathetically, cowering as she rose with triumphant smugness.

The female colleague nearby looked at me with a mix of disappointment and condescension (well, it *felt* like that, it might have been indigestion or disinterest, to be fair). It stopped me in my tracks. Yes, I understood that these dolls were anatomically impossible and in many respects unhelpful, but should we not have allowed her to have them in her toy box AT ALL? Should I have tried to steer her away from all things glitter and sparkly and fuchsia and blush?

In class, I found myself clandestinely canvassing the Year 7 girls. Targeting the ones who weren't dripping in Rimmel, I casually (hard, when they were doing Pythagoras) brought the conversation around to 'Dolls you had when you were little'. And I lied – I said I was thinking about what to buy for my daughter's birthday and reminiscing about what I had played with when I myself was a girl (Sindy, btw). Here, I would like to be able to say they shared insightful and unexpectedly mature musings on how having 36 Bratz dolls in no way made them any less determined to be a chemical engineer. But they didn't – they just looked a bit scared.

By lunchtime, I was that molten mix of insecure and defensive. My parenting was very easily pushed off-kilter by a certain kind of woman. Back then my mothering confidence could be crushed like a damp finger painting in the bottom of a backpack. The women I wanted to be like were the very ones who could make me feel like crap. I felt so keenly that lack of couscous and piano-playing. So keenly, in fact, that I could silence my own instincts before these women had uttered the second syllable of their opinion. It's interesting that now, of course, I can see that some of them were not *always* that nice and, maybe, a little on the judgemental side. Had I listened to the students at the time, I would have got the measure more quickly – 'Oh my God, Miss Forsyth? TOTAL bitch!' Often I was looking in the wrong direction for solidarity and wisdom.

Later, I am immersed with my wider family (the direction I should have looked in more often, frankly). They are cooing over my daughter and her increasing pile of gifts. She has been given an enormous sketchpad and some paints – tiny watercolours that she would demolish in one sitting – and she is lit up. As is her Nannie, who instilled in my girl her love of daubing. They set about sketching fairies and composing the story they will then write around their ethereal characters. They've been making these stories together since her chubby hand could pick up a pencil. The room is loud and smells of icing. The central heating hums and I notice, as I melt into its comfort and the third cuppa, that the birthday girl has, by now, disappeared. I go to her room and tap the door gently, pushing it open to find her sat at her new desk, shoulders back and a stern look on her face. Around her are sat a number of players from her team box: teddies, Lego models, Play Doh characters of her own making, and there they are: the Barbies.

'What are you playing, baby?' I ask.

She picks up a wooden hammer and bashes it down. 'I am being a very good and important judge, making very important DECISIONS!' she booms, triumphant.

I look around her room – her dozens of books, the reams and reams of paper that have captured pieces of her huge imagination, the pools of sand on her carpet from her fossil kits (she wants to be a palaeontologist because she loves a dig and a reveal, this kid).

There IS pink but she is *all* colours of the rainbow: no single toy, no particular game, and certainly no brand or shade of magenta will stymie the stories she wants to tell and the pictures she wants to paint. What she needed was for her mother to get over herself (frankly) and realise that she was already filling her daughter's world with choices and stories of adventure. Barbie could be an experimental physicist or own a pet-grooming parlour. And so could my girl. Who knows? Meantime, she would be the judge of that: it's all in the game.

A year or so later, I am sat near a group of Year 9 students, who are kicking around their options for GCSEs.

Katy: I hate science, though. I don't mind biology too much.

Sarah: I like doing the drawings of the plants. Pig's trotters, though – oh my LIFE!

Scott: I like Ingerlish and drawlin.

Katy: You mean English and art, Scott?

Scott: Yeah, but only if I gets Mr Crooke – he's a legend. He let my sister's class smoke in his lesson.

Sarah: That is utter CRAP! That's been going round for ages but it's a lie.

Scott: It actually happened, so piss off!

Katy: But I don't know if I want to do biology at A level, though.

Scott: I'm not doing A levels so I'm going for what'll be the biggest doss. I'm going on the sites anyway.

Sarah: What's that?

Scott: Building sites. I can go straight into that so this is all pointless. I could do science if I wanted, though – boys are brilliant at that.

Katy: Some are, some aren't. What's photosynthesis?

Scott: It's plants and the sun and shit – and a really long equation. Most boys are good at science but girls aren't usually that good at it. They can do food tech, though. Get the tea on!

Sarah: Oh, my actual fucking CHRIST, Scott! It's not the 1950s no more, you know.

Scott: I'm jokin'. And you don't need to tell me that – my mum's a plumber.

Katy: More girls are doctors, I read that somewhere. More go to medical school. I think you need A level biology for that.

Sarah: Do you wanna be a doctor, hun? You're so pretty, though . . .

Katy: My mum said I could be a model, yeah. At least then I could have kids.

Scott: So girls that are doctors don't have kids? I don't think that's true. I know our doctor's got kids cause she drops them off at Scouts. Well, when I used to go. Obviously I don't go now; it's lame.

Katy: Yeah, they do, but it must be hard trying to be like a doctor in a hospital and a mum. I wanna be home with my kids.

Sarah: I totally don't know what I want to do.

Katy: You are SO good at art, though. You've got to take that at least.

Scott: I'm doing it – with Crookes.

Sarah: What jobs can you do, though? I mean, not many people are artists for work, are they?

Katy: Of course they are! Look at that woman with the Tampax in her bed.

Scott: Tracey Amen.

Katy: Yeah, *her*! She makes all this art, not paintings, but it's her stuff and people really like it and she makes loads of money.

Sarah: I've seen her on the telly. It's Emin, Scott.

Scott: Exactly what I just said.

Katy: My mum said she should make more effort with how she looks.

Sarah: I'm not being funny, Kate, right? But your mum is a bit over the top about women's looks. That Tracey looks a bit tired but she is *so* cool and look how rich she is! I quite like how she looks, to be honest. She looks edgy, how an artist like, should look. Like they have something they want to say and they are knackered out trying to say it.

You *are both* good at science, though. You could be a good-looking doctor, Katy. Scott could be like a clever but well ugly scaffolder.

> *When I say to you, there is nobody like me, and there never was, that is a statement I want every woman to feel and make about themselves.*
>
> Lady Gaga, talking in the *LA Times*, 13 December, 2009

SO . . .

- I can see where the anti-pink campaign is coming from and what they are worried about. But it's really nuts to get fixated on a colour that can, in many mediums, be beautiful and fun. It's a COLOUR.

- The more important issue is when toys are produced and targeted to gender. Separate colouring books: boys (blue: diggers and cars) and girls (pink: tiaras and kittens). You know who you are, major high-street stationer. Or of course those playkits that have decided boys will only aspire to be footballers and girls to be nurses. Laugh at this stuff, with your kids, from early on. Create a narrative of the world that highlights just what nonsense this is: 'HA! *Look* at this! As *IF* all that girls are excited about is dressing up and babies!' And say that to sons *and* daughters in equal measure. This is setting the scene for individuality to emerge confidently but also for each gender to challenge gender stereotypes for themselves as they grow.

- CHOICES. You don't have to be Billy Elliot's dad to put off a child who is burning to try something they think might meet with your disapproval. It often seeps out of us without us realising, but they can feel it nonetheless. We see more and more 'girls doing boys' stuff' such as success on the football field, but it's happening much more slowly the other way round. Parents of both genders need to make sure that choice is something they talk about as a family, introducing ideas for hobbies and activities equally to boys and girls. Their interests change as they do, but they need to feel comfy to pick what excites them and try it on for size. My girl did dance classes when she was little, and as I write has just started playing football at university. I don't think my boy was harbouring a desire to do jazz tap, but what I know for sure is that he knows me and his dad would have been cool with that. I would have been off-the-scale THRILLED, let's be honest!

- Fiction is where it's at: we all know how important reading is and how life-enhancing (and at times life-*saving*) literature can be. With our girls, we can spread before them the bounty of stories that celebrate female heroes across the ages. The authors themselves become extraordinary people in the eyes of even tiny girls. Could J. K. Rowling *be* any more wonderful in her work and the way she leads her life? And now, the quite brilliant Lena Dunham and her body of work that is enabling young women of this generation to feel understood and empowered. Real role models and amazing stories: immerse your girl in them so she can feel all the possibilities and eschew the limitations that ye olde patriarchy still cling to desperately.

♦ Speaking of real, what is real anyway? In all the conversations we will have with our girls around beauty in the media and the jobs women do within it, there is so much opportunity to shatter the myths. In the film *The Women*, we see 13-year-old Molly talking to her mother's best friend, a magazine editor played by Annette Bening. She unhappily implores, 'I want to look like the women in your magazine' to which Bening replies, somewhat wearily and a little guiltily, 'Honey, *THEY* don't look like the women in my magazines!' Similarly, if our kids see a scantily clad megastar like Rihanna and, as with Caitlin Moran's kids, we suggest she could do with a cardigan, we can be fairly sure we're onto a good thing. Shaggable can be comfortable too.

♦ Point being, your girl can be finding a cure for cancer as well as searching for the perfect halter-neck top.

'Born This Way' – Lady Gaga. Of COURSE! The perfect way to complete this chapter.

Chapter 10

I Want My Boy to be a Floppy-haired Poet (He Wants to Play in the NFL): Navigating Gender Stereotypes With Your Son

Raising *your* son

Vik

My son was my first child – my shadow for four years until his sister landed, in the night, while he slept in the room next door in his flannelette Tigger pyjamas. He strolled in after all the drama, blissfully unaware, to see the sleeping dot by my side. 'She's nice,' he said before heading off for Weetabix. Like his father, he is a man of few but often well-placed words.

He was the easiest of small boys: loving, snuggly, a self-contained chap who loved puddles, painting and Daddy and me. I wanted to hit the pause button at around three years old, then again at ten, before he went off to buildings full of grown-ups that were not me, and OTHER BOYS. I decided he was a *deeply sensitive* fella and worried desperately that anyone might be unkind to him. In fact he (you're there before me) was a standard robust kid, making his way through friendship traffic with adequate bumpers. He just did it quietly, at his own pace, and always had pals. At around thirteen, he made the turn; the almost overnight slimming of chubby cheeks and deepening of vowel sounds. I was simultaneously thrilled and terrified.

When you are embryo cooking, you picture your child in a million different ways: a kid kaleidoscope. Their face, their laugh . . . how they will grow and who they will be. Will they reject couscous? Will they cling to you shyly on the first day of nursery, or go in and push over the really small kid? Might they have a penchant for reptiles and in which case, have to be put up for adoption? That sort of thing . . .

Pondering this with the wider family, 'future visioning' came up. We had a family friend who had recently come out after two marriages to men and so we kicked around potential sexual orientation as well as careers; it was all up for speculative grab. And a welcome break from the real-life struggles of the Big Brother house, frankly. My sister peeled the wrapper off a nostalgic Curly Wurly and said 'God, I'd LOVE it if H was gay! I would always be the most important woman in his life then, wouldn't I?' Our mother countered, 'No, because that is already me.'

In our wider family, it would be fair to say, the men are fairly traditional – loving and caring, brothers, fathers, sons. They are more comfortable on the football touchline than with a broadsheet byline. And to be honest, one or two are likely to stray into lazy, low-level sexism, if left unchecked.

The powerful narrative of 'laddism' was one that my sisters and friends feared. The doctrine of macho and all of the deflating and often damaging messages it sends to growing boys about what being a man is supposed to be about. I didn't want my boy to get sucked into that vortex: big shot, action hero, joker, buffoon, strong and silent, commitment-phobe . . . UGH! How to challenge all of *that* as he grew?

Quietly, I hoped the 'deep sensitivity' I convinced myself defined my boy would translate into an active eschewing of all things full-on macho and instead he would become a pensive, poetry-reading fella (with an impossibly floppy fringe from which he would periodically emerge and ask existential questions). OK, I know, I can be SUCH a prat sometimes. I worried, though. I feared the 'less than helpful' male voices in our collective families would diminish our careful nurturing of the values of gender equality and mutual respect. Cultivating fringes and a love of literature wasn't *exactly* going to help foster all of that though, was it? One stereotype doesn't trump another.

More than anything we wanted him to feel happy in his own skin, whatever his heart and loins were telling him, and despite what the culture around him was yelling (or the slightly pervy uncles were cracking jokes about). Not wanting to lose your boy from your life is one thing and I got the hell over myself on that, but him not feeling lost within his own life – that's everything. There is nothing more central to our happiness than feeling safe enough to be who we are and love whom we want.

I couldn't insist on mittens here; I could only counter some of the chillier aspects of adolescence from the warmth of home. Not that he seemed to ever need it. He survived happily despite me checking him hourly for signs of emotional distress – 'I'm FINE, Mum' (I still do this when I'm feeling vulnerable, to both my kids; it's insane.) What he did need was the relationship with his father to take a different shape as he grew into a young man, without my constant interference. Reader, epic fail here! Like a lot of mothers, I leant in too much and too often to their moments, thinking they needed

mediating – they didn't. It's a different bond and it needed space
to breathe. I had to get to the other side of that time to realise this
so I offer it up as a salutary lesson. Thank Christ they ignore me a
great deal! My eternal gratitude too, to my gentle, strong and lovely
husband, who enabled my son to have a childhood immersed in the
very best qualities of not just masculinity but humanity as well. A
man who can watch Formula 1, read war novels, cry at a romcom,
lust over Nigella and then get the tea on. He mends things too, which
I know is a MASSIVE gender stereotype but it's dead handy, man
(see what I did there!). He's his own man, not at the mercy of the
view of others or in need of constant affirmation from his male peers.
What else could have been more important for our boy to see?

Currently, in this year of 2015 and at the age of twenty-five, he works
in technical recruiting, swoons over one of the female leads in the
US series *Entourage* (which is pretty sexist, to be honest, so I watch
with him and offer a helpful critique, with snacks, for which he's
terribly grateful, as you can imagine). He has no working knowledge
of Keats. Which frankly, I couldn't give less of a shit about. I like him
ENORMOUSLY. He likes HIMSELF . . .

His late nan was so disappointed in her collective brood: 'Not one
of 'em plays an instrument or is queer. I can't *believe* it!' Yes, with
a straight face that was delivered. But as the words tumbled out,
she practically shone with the enormous pride she felt for their utter
individuality. As her grandboys grew into men, and plucked her
from her increasingly frail toes to their arms and onto the dance
floor, I saw emerging in our family another set of men; embracing
and enjoying the camaraderie and connectedness of their masculine
worlds but stopping, frequently, and with palpable and reverential
awe, to listen to and love the women in their lives. ALL our voices
shape them. I see young men who have had their vulnerable moments
within a culture that thrusts images at them of what success is
supposed to look like for dudes. I see them try to work it all out,
falter now and again, but then have some fun and lean back in with

comfort to the stories, old and new, of their brethren. I still wince at some of the uncles, mind. But they have at times been the exact ballast our boys needed.

I hear them make the odd joke about tits. But then *I* make jokes about tits. They can be very funny, can't they, tits?

> *I know I'm not the handiest guy, but I'm still a man and I want to be able to look out into my yard and say, 'There's a little bit of me in that princess castle'.*
>
> *Mitchell*, Modern Family

SO . . .

♦ Brené Brown, a researcher and writer, did some work on vulnerability and shame. A TED (Technology, Entertainment, Design) talk catapulted her to international fame. In her book, *Daring Greatly*, Brené recounts a conversation she had at a book signing with a man who approached her with his wife and daughters. He asked Brené why she didn't talk about men in her work and she told him well, that was because she had only studied women. He replied, 'Well, that's convenient.' And went on, 'We have shame, we have deep shame, but when we reach out and tell our stories, we get the emotional crap beat out of us.' He added, 'And before you say anything about those mean fathers and those coaches and those brothers and those bully friends, my wife and three daughters, the ones who you just signed the books for, they had rather see me die on top of my white horse than have to watch me fall off.' Then he just walked away . . .

♦ It is at best, disingenuous, and at worst, lethal, to suggest that gender stereotyping doesn't do damage to boys and men – it does. The under-thirty-five male suicide rate in the UK is a statistic that should enable a conversation not just about mental health but how we raise our boys. But some unhelpful voices, on social media in particular, keep shutting down this conversation. It's maddening. We have SO much to talk about here.

♦ 'Man up, man cub' trips off the tongue into our lexicon and before we know it, into some of the subtle messages the most mindful and careful parents give to little fellas about what masculinity is supposed to look like.

♦ Look at the small chap in front of you. Does he like rough and tumble? Does he run at you like a steam train, whooping as you lift him and whirl him around by his armpits? Or does he wince, stiffen or go along with it with a pinched smile because 'Daddy likes rugby'? Take your cue from him in terms of what he *clearly* enjoys and feels comfortable with in terms of types of play and toys.

♦ Try not to adopt a 'blue lens' and direct your son to only look at the world through it, pointing out stereotypical stuff such as construction and action. Because when boys are unconsciously steered towards what we think they will be into (and don't beat yourself up that you have those pre-conceived notions) we run the risk that we won't nurture in them the talents they have innately rumbling simply because no one offered up those possibilities.

♦ Perhaps we should neither discourage nor encourage any interest hotly. See what shows up in their emerging personalities and never say no to anything based on gender. When you see their eyes light up, THEN ramp up your enthusiasm.

♦ Don't agonise over the unhelpful voices. From early on, be brave when you feel you can and build up. Put your wee fellow in a yellow or pink baby-gro – Grandma won't die! And gradually, you will feel able to make challenges to what people expect from you as you parent a boy. Encourage him to be a nurturer, not a superhero. No one expects to hear that around a boy so much. He can still wear his pants over his tights, though – that is always a marvellous thing.

♦ Qualities and passion are what we yearn to grow in our kids, rooted firmly in the ideas of life being a buffet of choice. Right?

♦ So, back to vulnerability . . . Well, that's just courage. Courage to connect with others, create and occasionally fail. When we raise our boys to be feminists, we are helping men into the world who can talk about fear, *without* fear. Men who would neither beat the emotional crap out of themselves nor anyone else in their lives; men who know they are not expected to ride any damn white horse or indeed stay on one . . . Unless of course they choose *dressage*, in which case, how LOVELY!

♦ Feminism isn't one-upmanship; equality is equality, whether it's a woman's right to equal pay or a man's right to celebrate his nurturing side. So let's stop pitching the one against the other: we're not opposing camps.

Songs In The Key of Life *by Stevie Wonder is one of the greatest albums ever. You have to love it, there is NO choice and if ever there was a glorious celebration of growing up and adventures, it's 'I Wish'!*

Chapter 11

Respect Your Elders or Rage Against the Machine? When One-size-fits-all Conventions Just Don't Fit

Raising kids who question, but don't always conform

AI

It's fair to say that Queen Victoria and her crew had a bit of an issue with sex. But it's not that she didn't *like* it – far from it (she and Albert banged out nine children in fourteen years). She just wasn't at all happy about the way some of her subjects were choosing to do it.

We all know this about the Victorians – or we think we do: they were frigid. In fact, the work of French historian Michel Foucault on the sexual mores of the era reveals a complex, layered and changing relationship with sex and sexuality throughout the decades of Victoria's reign. The focus of it all, he argued, was not the condemnation or the suppression of sex, but its *regulation*. Victorian bureaucracy, it seems, extended even into the bedroom.

Significant amounts of time and money were devoted to the categorisation of those aspects of sex that were deemed acceptable and those to be regarded as a societal evil – specifically, masturbation, prostitution and (a brand new psychological 'condition', coined largely as a result of Queen Victoria's abhorrence of its prevalence among the male aristocracy): homosexuality.

By the latter decades of the nineteenth century, respectable married men were advised to practice 'self-vigilance' – trying not to – as often as they could. The scientific principle behind this argued that the body was a closed system of energy: expend energy with your 'nocturnal emissions' and you would effectively 'run low' on power for a while. You would jeopardise your ability to excel in Court, the Commons or the boardroom the following day. But for adolescent boys, yet to develop self-control, help was at hand in the form of a variety of brutal steel Y-fronts, some even bearing spikes designed to *discourage* those nasty nocturnal stiffies and keep them bright and breezy and ready to learn the next day.

Meanwhile women were confidently declared to be less commonly prone to sexual voracity, as reflected in the popular British ditty:

Hogamus higamus

Men are polygamous

Higamus hogamus

Women are monogamous.

But women were far from left out of all that new medical *fun*. A similarly spectacular piece of scientific misinformation prompted the (male) head of many a well-to-do Victorian household to check obsessively for *evidence* that his wife and daughters' menstrual cycles were regular: bloodied rags were to be presented for inspection on a monthly basis.

A delayed cycle, it was argued, created an excess of blood. And if it wasn't being released from the body once a month in the normal fashion, where exactly *was* it going? Surely, it had to go *somewhere*? Its only course, it was decided (by men, naturally), was the brain, where it would result in another newly defined psychological condition, this time experienced only by women (and only by those women with an irregular cycle): *hysteria.*

One other truly remarkable consequence was born of the combined impact of these two Victorian principles: the endemic terror of irregular periods (with the associated risk of hysteria), coupled with the widely accepted scientific *truth* that a sexual appetite was an almost exclusively male phenomenon.

In order to release the cerebral tension caused by a late period, girls of delicate persuasion were frequently taken – by their *mothers* – to their physician, at considerable expense, in order that he perform 'pelvic massage'. Proof of the sense of all this, if proof were needed, could be found in the audible paroxysms emanating from behind docs' doors all over Britain, Europe and America throughout the late-nineteenth century. Once or twice a month, teenage girls and young married women were queuing in waiting rooms for a medicinal, prophylactic handjob.

Let's just let that hang there a while . . .

The problem was that while the practice of physician-assisted 'paroxysm' was keeping many doctors in business, it was also playing havoc with the poor chaps' hands. In order to ease this large-scale, occupational RSI, one Dr Joseph Mortimer Granville invented an alarming-looking contraption, which, once a young hysteric was securely strapped inside, would do the job mechanically – a massive, sit-on vibrator, then.

It's all messed up, isn't it?

My point is, sooner or later, we all reach an understanding that there's a *difference* between a widely held convention and that all-important inner voice that quietly asserts: *this is wrong. This feels wrong.* What matters most of all is that innate sense of justice; our kids have to tune in to that if they are going to stand a chance of living robust, honest lives. We need to help them come to see that sometimes, conventions need challenging and that occasionally, they're just plain wrong. Because the trouble with conventions is that the more you investigate their genesis, the more you come to see that they are extensively defined by the dominant forces of the age.

Take the moment of our birth, for instance. In any maternity room across the world, someone generally announces, 'You have a daughter', or 'It's a boy' or something similar. A self-contained, tidy statement of fact, it makes *sense*, providing us all with a working mental association. We instantly take comfort from the logic of this information. But that's not the way it's always been – in fact, it's not even how everyone does it today.

We haven't always needed to define everyone according to ticked boxes.

Before white Europeans rocked up and forcefully asserted the superiority of their own moral code, Native American tribes had an entirely different attitude to gender, separate and distinct from sexuality or morality. The Navajo, for instance, identify people according to two distinct aspects of what makes them who they are: their physical body and their spirit. A Navajo *asdzaan* is biologically a woman and spiritually female, and will therefore function socially as a female. *Dilbaa* are biologically female but, on account of their masculine spirit, function socially as male. Similarly, *hastiin* members of the Navajo community have a masculine spirit aligned with a male body, whereas the *nádleehí* are biologically male and socially, spiritually female.

What's even more significant is that in common with many other Native American nationalities, Navajo culture sees *dilbaa* and *nádleehí* members of the community as more spiritually in tune with their elders and ancestors. They are revered; other members of the community turn to them for spiritual and moral guidance.

In fact, there are countless cultures peppering every continent and every era of human history that do not adhere to those two basic categories – boy girl; man woman. That's a degree of fluidity that our modern, industrialised, bureaucratic society *cannot* handle, defined as it is by paper-pushers, box-tickers and neat-freaks. Who are we to shout down those who identify themselves in a way that falls outside the boundaries of our convention?

There is *always* another way of seeing things; there is *always* an alternative view. Discussion of ideas and the evolution of conventions is how the human race has *always* rolled. We need to be creating childhoods filled with the space to explore, the freedom to question and the expectation that change is inevitable. In fact, that change is where it's at: it's progress, it's survival, it's our only hope.

> *Honey, there is no one right way to eat cannelloni.*
>
> *Alyssa Brugman*, Alex As Well

SO . . .

♦ A child that swims against the tide of convention is a gift. But s/he is also a child who may well experience choppy waters so be a constant in their life. Neither encourage nor discourage, *never* judge and certainly, don't feel the need to stop what hurts no one. Childhood is all about behaviour that doesn't conform to adult conceptions of stereotypes: step back.

♦ You'll be making assumptions — fast-forwarding fifteen years and painting a picture of what your wee 'un is going to look like, talk like, behave like. And chances are, what you're imagining won't be feeling comfortable so cut it out. Seriously, stop it. Whatever you're picturing, it's an *invention* and it's helping no one. Besides, fifteen years down the line it will be their world every bit as much as it is ours. Who are we to judge?

♦ Read Cheryl Kilodavis's beautiful picturebook, *My Princess Boy.* And then make everyone you know read it too. It's the enchanting story of her son, Dyson, who plays just like any other child — in the park, up a tree, with his brother — he just prefers to do it in a dress.

Dyson began expressing a preference for female clothing from the age of two and his parents at first 'redirected' him — toy trucks, adventure books for boys, you know the stuff. Until one Hallowe'en when Dyson wanted to dress up as a princess. As they began to resist, their older son, Cody, said simply, 'Why can't you let him be happy?' And that's when his parents saw it: this was only a problem for the grown-ups. The kids were just busy being themselves.

Dyson's father, Dean, is extremely clear, telling a news programme in the US in 2011, 'It's not contagious. He's just a kid like any other kid. He plays the Chequers, he plays in the trees; he just likes to do it in a dress. Big deal.'

These are different times we live in: we're better. And we're better *because* we're starting to figure out that we have to *listen* to our kids. They're better at this stuff than we are.

♦ In Jonathan Skurnik's short documentary film, *The Family Journey: Raising Gender Nonconforming Children*, one contributing father says of his child, quite simply, 'I learned to trust her instincts on this.' And that's it, isn't it? If we've done the groundwork, the stuff that *really* matters, the stuff about developing a robust sense of themselves, knowing there's a solid core of love and acceptance within their family; if we've raised kind, questioning, honest and empathetic kids with a good heart and an innate sense of justice then we've done the hard part. Then it's just a case of learning to step back and trust their instincts. Because their instincts will be sound and their future a wonderful adventure. So, breathe!

I don't ask that you teach everyone around me about sex and gender and sexuality, but if you could teach them about empathy I would greatly appreciate it. Treat others how you want to be treated, it's that simple.

Lori Duron, Raising My Rainbow

Let's stop pretending that we have all the answers, because when it comes to gender, none of us is fucking omniscient.

Kate Borstein, Gender Outlaws: The Next Generation

What we need here is something to take focus OFF the fear for long enough to refocus on the bliss of watching your own child make turns you could never have anticipated, to challenge things that have never occurred to us to challenge. Your kids are fabulous, so trust them. Be brave enough to trust them. If you need a bit of help finding the courage, have a listen to Lady Gaga, 'The Queen'.

Chapter 12

Help! I Think My 12-year-old Daughter Wants to be a Nail Technician

Raising your nerve as kids explore their tribes

Vik

It was the year of the Jane Norman bag. The clothing store was churning out black PVC bags, bearing their logo in a variety of colours. It struck a chord with my daughter's peer group and soon practically every girl in Years 7, 8 and 9 had one in her possession, crammed with Impulse and copies of *Private Peaceful*. And no doubt the dashed hopes of 12-year-old boys, too.

I have to say I was shitting myself at this point. Having worked in secondary education since the mid-1990s, I was unhelpfully far too up to speed on the tribal nature and huge pressure on both boys and girls. The Spice Girls had hollered 'Girl Power!' but it hadn't translated into anything like a helpful, empowering message to young people (they just said 'Girl Power!' a lot). So for my girl, I was anxious. She had nice friends and loved school. Tick. But she was moving quickly and with determination towards pouting and ridiculously tight 'Miss Sexy' black trousers. These slacks of sin so outraged the community they ended up on the front page of the local paper, as the new head of the comp declared them banned. The reportage was hilarious and I went into full-on 'FFS, the suburbs' mode. But my baby was dropping a hip in early selfies. No *way* was this happening! Next, she would be hanging with girls who painted on their eyebrows and I would kill myself. I put her in Doc Martens from 18 months old, for crying out loud; she owed me.

It would be fair to say I overreacted here and there. I managed, despite my professional experience to the contrary, to convince myself that she was about to take an almighty big turn socially that would result in her becoming something like . . . *a hairdresser.* She would go the way many of the girls I went to school with: babies and blow-dries done at home for a fiver. Just a few years before, I had been working with girls in the same school. I had supported them to make applications for hair and beauty courses and been thrilled when they got in and made a success of it. But my girl, well, she was capable of more, so she had to fulfil her potential, right? Too much Lycra and lippy one minute, pregnant and absolutely not being a human rights lawyer the next . . . I could hardly *breathe* with anxiety. (Reading that back, I am choking on shame at my stupidity and snobbery.)

I can't honestly remember how I steered that time now and what I said to her. I was working crazy hard and distracted (a blessing for her) and I hope keeping it cool on the surface, if not underneath. My steady hand-on-the-tiller husband probably did a lot of 'She will be fine, babe', but I do remember a conversation I had with an ex-colleague. An intimidating teacher who had two boys, mostly raised solo in a boho flat in the most expensive, arty part of the city, she had pals called Theo and Faraday, that sort of thing. Anyway, at school she pushed the kids hard for Oxbridge. She was all about the bright buttons and deeply scathing/cruel about 'those special needs children' that I had to discuss with her. We weren't exactly kindred spirits. But on a rare work night out, slightly smashed, she told me: 'You just have to hold your nerve. They are going to be who they are going to be. You've had a hand in that, now you wait.' It stunned me that she was so laissez-faire. What? Just see how it *goes*? And do what in the meantime? Have joint manicures? No way, my daughter was getting Naomi Wolf and The Greer: breakfast, dinner, tea.

But I came to realise she was right; of bleedin' course she was right. My girl had some incredible role models: her aunts, her grandmothers, my friends and even beauty therapists and hairdressers. And before not too long, thank God, Caitlin Moran. I needed to feel safe that her exploration of femininity, in all its necessary hues, was something she was going to do (as I myself had) and was completely brilliant, sometimes achingly rough, but one where me keeping my shit in perspective would be helpful.

SMALL PAUSE FOR THOUGHT HERE: As *if* an interest in beauty and fashion couldn't lead to a highly fulfilling career and was in some way a lesser life pursuit! What *CRAP*! Some of the smartest women I admire most in the world are the greatest oracles on looking after your face as well as your soul, the writer Sali Hughes (absolutely marvellous broad) being the greatest exponent of this with her whip-smart wisdom, sweary wit and life-changing advice on skin.

What I needed to help my girl realise is how you can enjoy all types of connections with all types of pals: mates with whom you can lie upside down on your bed and talk about the BIG LIFE QUESTIONS and then mates that you can stand with in Boots for hours and dick about deciding on Barry M eyeshadows.

So my girl navigated her way through the politics and pressures of the early teens on her own steam, with some half-arsed, largely unhelpful input from me. Eventually she eschewed Jane Norman, just as she grew out of a lot of other stuff. Throughout she had fun, tears and was relentlessly glorious (though I would have not have used those *exact* words at the time). She made friends with girls and boys who were different characters and wanted different things. She had a burning sense of equality and a total intolerance of injustice.

When she was around fifteen, I fessed up to her. I told her how scared I was that she was going to slide into a social tribe where her aspirations might be different to what I had envisaged. That I wanted so much more for her than the women I grew up with had – exciting work, travel, non-abusive husbands. I reiterated my now-infamous speech of 'Don't, I beg you, spend £20K on a wedding. It's only a few *HOURS*! Call me from a beach somewhere, barefoot and in love, saying, "Mum, I'm married!" That's if you do it at all, because it's cool if you don't. I will *never* wear a peach hat.'

I had to see how it went. And meantime, listen, mop up, get to know her mates, have them here all the soddin' time (just as my brilliant Ma had done for us) and tell her often that she could do absolutely anything she wanted to do in the future and that no test, exam, or pair of trousers was going to set any of that story in stone.

She had power, my girl, and there was more to come.

> *Whatever you choose, however many roads you travel, I hope that you choose not to be a lady. I hope you will find some way to break the rules and make a little trouble out there. And I also hope that you will choose to make some of that trouble on behalf of women.*
>
> Nora Ephron, in her Commencement Address to the students of Wellesley College, 1996

SO . . .

♦ Friendships are tribal at this stage of the game and for both boys
and girls this can be rough when they're working out who they
are and what they're into. Or they don't feel safe yet to let out
who is cooking inside. Of course we all went through it so we can
empathise, but our own stories will only soothe so far; we can be
largely irrelevant to our children in our nostalgia. *They* are in the
moment each day and they want to belong real bad – they long
to be mates with kids that they don't actually really like or have
connections that are doing them no soddin' good whatsoever. Or at
least that's what us parents think at the time. It feels very urgent and
necessary when you're them and you're in Period 4 physics. My now
21-year-old daughter reflects, 'You get to a point where you know
what you want from school and beyond, and you move towards the
friends who want the same.'

♦ At the very core of feminism is perspective-taking – the art of being
able to understand others and respecting that we have an equal right
to roll as we choose. We have to see their perspective now. Hear it;
really, *really* listen to it in whatever shouty or fragile way it appears.
The scariest moments are often the most teachable.

♦ Reason, season and a lifetime: in our own experience of friendships,
people come and go. It's inevitable. Your home, whatever the shape
and size of the adult contingent, needs to be a place where that
narrative is palpable, where your kids feel the presence of your own
friendships around *you* and indeed them, but also hear you reflect
when those relationships falter, change or end. Often that's messy,
yet if they absorb the message from you that people shape us but
don't define us, they can begin to understand that graciously and
respectfully moving within and beyond friendships is a formative and
fundamental part of life. So maybe try *not* to behave like a petulant
14-year-old on Facebook with an old school friend who has four
degrees and a house in Tuscany. We as women, men, mothers
and fathers are still constantly reshaping who we are through our

connections and experiences. Show them that vulnerability and getting people wrong is all in the game.

♦ Don't interfere with or contribute to their conversations unless *expressly* invited. It's at best unhelpful, at worst rather sad for a parent to need to be in the minutiae of what young people are sharing. As Al says in Chapter 16, you can't know everything about your child and nor should you. Never was this truer than now. If you take the temperature of the group from what they are saying, most of the time you will be wrong anyway. It's banter; it's their vernacular . . . And it changes.

♦ I overheard a woman the other day saying gleefully to her 13-year-old daughter, 'I thought Amelia was being a total bitch to you the other day. I wouldn't invite her to your party!' Now I don't know the backstory but I do know the look on the girl's face. Step OFF! If there's an issue, and you've set up a 'listening with snacks clinic – open twenty-four hours', then they will let you know if Amelia is a problem for *them*. Any human of any age would rather own their 'stuff' than have someone else tell them what they think their problems are and what they should do about it.

I guess if I had a bit of script to share from back then it would run something like this:

Baby, liking other people is the easy bit. Liking yourself takes work because all the time we have worries and all the time we see things on telly and around us that urge us to compare ourselves to others. That's mostly because they want us to buy something and it's all, actually, rubbish. Be kind to yourself, be kind to others, but don't take any crap because you think you're not enough. We are ALL enough. You, you are a zillion kinds of wonderful!

'In My Mind' by Amanda Palmer is a triumphant ode to the internal dreams and hopes we all have and the wrestle for our identity.

Chapter 13

P45s, PTAs and Pesto: Parenting While In and Out of Work – And In and Out of Love With Work
Raising kids who aren't afraid to fail

Vik

You know you're good at reframing when you are sat sobbing over situations vacant in a Little Chef, miles from home, and you get a text from your old boss saying, 'How's the new job working out?' to which you reply, 'Awesome! I've NEVER been happier! How's you? Still slogging it out at that hellish shower?'

OK, good at barefaced lying then.

I'd been miserable in a job that had allowed me to forge a great career over eight years. The all-women team I worked with were extraordinary broads and I loved them but I was coming to the end of my energies there. It was a charity and money was tight. As a manager, I was being squeezed.

So one surreal afternoon in December, I'm on autopilot with exhaustion at a conference in Leicester with rubbish biscuits, when I succumb to the seductive power of a hugely charismatic leader. She literally pummelled me with patchouli and relentless optimism. I had no chance. She plucked me.

Next minute (or so it felt) I'm wandering the grounds of a grand country house hotel while she tells me of all her plans for me, the empire-building, and the enormous fun and adventures we are going to have together. I lap it up.

At one point she steps away from me to take a call on her mobile. She thinks I can't hear, I suspect, but the wind direction betrays her: she is steely cold in tone. I don't know who she is talking to but I'm bloody glad it's not me. That same wind whips around me, chills me, scares me a bit. Then drops.

A few weeks later, I am heading from home to my first day, giddy with anticipation. This is going to be my moment, working for a creative genius – a freeing, highly edifying trip into the next chapter of my working life. Bring it on! *I will learn to breathe rather than eat my way through crises and I'll gladly embrace chanting or yoga. I am a fucking GODDESS!*

My induction went something like this: zero time with new boss. I made sandwiches for support workers. I may have nipped to Sainsburys at one point. I picked up some interesting and rather worrying gossip around 'what *really* goes down here'. I started to wonder about this empire, this field of dreams I thought I was about to skip gaily through. But hey, first day, right? Always feels utterly rudderless and scary. I text my old team 'It's going to be good this! Not a spreadsheet in sight, lads!'

It's late, and I finally see the charismatic one.

'OK, so I need to tell you about the people who are unhappy with your appointment' she beams, grasping my hand warmly

There follows a terrifying tirade. Senior colleagues – people with whom I needed to build a relationship – are gradually crushed as I am told of all their failings and neuroses, all in the manner of 'it's best to know up front isn't it, and I couldn't be more thrilled you are with us!!' I start to wonder, is this 'creative genius' actually just an egotistical tyrant, wearing rather a lot of pleasant scarves? I think I may be well and truly plucked.

So, how do I tell the old man and kids how the first day went then . . .?

Headlines from the next twelve months

Countless, miserable days on the roads, fighting every fibre of my being to turn around and go home

Panic attacks

A clinical dependence on Caramacs

A couple of life-affirming allies made (there is *always* sisterhood, everywhere)

Fast poo situation in a swimming pool . . .

An evening in a 'wellness circle' with a colleague, who told me a ghost called Sheila was sat on my lap. Some pee came out of me while suppressing laughter (she thought I was deeply moved)

An even more memorable evening where the great leader made an exhausted team of colleagues watch a DVD montage she'd made of her daughter, on to which she had done her own voiceover. It was midnight and we had to go all the way through to the end to hear her say, breathily, 'This child will inspire the whole WORLD'. I laugh *now*

A husband, frightened

A tiny nervous breakdown

A new job

Medicated, watching Cash in the Attic, I spoke to my daughter. I'd told the kids I'd made a big leap and as it turned out, a big old mistake. It had made me poorly because I thought I couldn't get back out from behind the mistake and I would end up working the tills at Lidl. Not that there's anything wrong with shop work, mind you, I was quick to point out, eager to be, um, middle-class in my sensitivities and delivery. Meantime, babies, I am home and able to be super-creative with courgettes on our limited budget, so fear not.

My son had been relaxed and confident in my ability to find work before the new job offer landed. Not given to panic by nature, a steady and at times unknowable man-child. My daughter, then nineteen, anxious and watching me closely, was inching nearer. So we talked.

'Mum, you do realise she was clearly barking? I don't think you had a dog's chance really. I mean, the *endless* yoga? Seriously? You can't run a company on that kinda shit!' she said. And I cried, suddenly and copiously, and she was briefly worried she'd said the wrong thing so I wiped my snot theatrically on her sleeve, citing payback for years of her vom and bogies, and we laughed and talked about dreams and ambitions and things not working out.

I had no answers, but I had some fresh experiences and I laid them out for her to consider as she stood on the cusp of her own working world.

My kids have had me at home, working very locally and at the gates every day, and away for days at a time in a national role. They have watched me give interviews on breakfast telly, winced as they stumbled into my study and saw the Velcro penises on my desk (for *TEACHING*, people), cried on the phone to me when I've been hundreds of miles away because Daddy got the wrong ketchup and was breaching their human rights by insisting they pick up their socks. They have had my beloved past and present colleagues as treasured adults in their own lives. They have watched me seethe, succumb and, occasionally, succeed in my working endeavours (and wobbled in the face of my fears and failures). They have seen their father do the very same. Although I am somewhat more melodramatic than him in my responses, I won't lie to you.

I have loved, in equal measure, my years at home when they were small and my years at work as they grew. Mindful that my choices, *our* choices as a family, shaped their emotional security through my presence, I was also deadly keen that they see me as a woman lit up by work and all the richer a mother to them for it. I had tales from the chalkface and then the road, informed opinions, experience and the ability to pay the mortgage (and I was remarkably relaxed about dirty socks). You'll need to ask them if I was any kind of a feminist role model. They'll laugh a lot first, mind, and then say deeply unkind and untrue things about how much I overreact.

It is not the critic who counts; not the woman* who points out how the strong woman* stumbles, or where the doer of deeds could have done them better. The credit belongs to the woman* who is actually in the arena, whose face is marred by dust and sweat and blood; who strives valiantly... who at the best knows in the end the triumph of high achievement, and who at the worst, if she* fails, at least fails while daring greatly, so that her* place shall never be with those cold and timid souls who neither know victory nor defeat.

Theodore Roosevelt, in a speech delivered to the
University of the Sorbonne, Paris, 1910

*OK, so we took a liberty: Roosevelt originally talked about dudes here, but he meant SHE too. Because, seriously, Eleanor? Badass broad, right there!

When it comes to getting that work–home balance right, there are no rules. It's a question of doing what needs doing, listening to your gut and feeling your way through it. Listen to a little bit of the great Ella Fitzgerald singing, 'It Ain't What You Do, It's the Way That You Do It'. She knew it, too.

SO . . .

♦ Work and kids: there is no script. The only certainty is you will feel all sorts of emotions and will make all sorts of choices, good and not so good. Some directed by financial necessity, others by ambition, some even by supposedly powerful gemstones. You never can tell.

♦ Always, in the living of it all, there are sound lessons for your kids to observe. And those are all around how you roll with the punches. How you decide that there is almost always something to be drawn from your triumphs as well as your failures at work – even when you feel battered and broken *and* poor. There are new people to know and there is learning about who and what to avoid in the future.

♦ Kids are being raised not knowing how to fail because we keep expecting perfection at school and into work choices. This is disastrous when it comes to feminism because women are expected to be perfect on *every* front, including their appearance. Women are pressured to look as though they are gliding on air through it all. It's disastrous when it comes to *people* because vulnerability is the key to EVERYTHING. Not being afraid to have a go is the way to find out who you are and what you want. So don't perfect yourself or them, just have a go at things. Even an eight-week stint in Curry's will have some merit. Possibly a lifelong aversion to purple and the general public, but still, rich tapestry, gas bill paid!

♦ When you have kids, there is a queue of voices telling you what you should do about work and motherhood. And look, here's us, doing the same. But maybe what we are saying is just this: you can do both. Most of us have no bloody choice anyway. But it's massively healthy for your kids to see you as this whole separate person to them, stimulated and earning. Yet there's no escaping you also need to be present in their lives. How that all looks for you, and your family, is YOUR call, dependent on your unique world. But it's not a flawless, fluid process; it's an inch-through, 'keep having a look at it all' stagger.

♦ You will feel guilt quite a lot. Because you often end up somewhere at the exact time when you feel you should be elsewhere. Perhaps you missed your son's judo class or you were late to a meeting because your child was in meltdown over the evil doctrine that is testing. But you can't win 'em all and the dilemmas are well documented: you are ENOUGH. So get the 'Von Tramps' out for a bit and feel better! Don't agonise in front of your kids too much – they probably know you feel shit and are likely to milk it in pursuit of extended bedtimes and hard cash, so just play a game together and stumble on, happily crappy.

♦ Controversy alert. Sometimes the very best parent is a temporarily absent one. If you have to go away for work, then do it with a spring in your step because raising kids can be really bloody dull and is always knackering, so being able to sod off is GOOD NEWS! For them and you. You are thrilled to then be home again and less likely to drink heavily at the prospect of recorder practice (suddenly you are deeply *keen*). They need to miss you and have stories in which you don't feature to tell you all about before 'Teeth. Now'. Having siblings as co-conspirators in your selfish absence is massively bonding for them. They are a very small gang who managed not to die while you were slurping Chilean Blanc at the Premier Inn in Worthing. Result: an all-round damn fine break from domestic tedium. And a Brucie Bonus: sometimes other grown-ups can sort your kids and their stuff out better than you can, especially teens and older relatives, so accept it. You ain't the *ubermeister*, kid!

♦ The narrative that's essential for kids to hear is one where there is parity of consideration and energy for the work choices of both parents if, of course, there are two in your gaff and they are a man and a woman. This building block to a fundamental understanding of feminism, home-grown and felt, paves the way for kids to know that there can – and must – be an equality of choice in work and life decisions for both genders: they have seen this, so they will carve it out for themselves, instinctively.

Chapter 14

FML: Growing Up in the Glare of Social Media
Raising kids with a healthy e-life

Al

One memorable evening, my daughter's mate, Anna, changed her Facebook profile picture to a selfie she'd taken in the pool on holiday.

She'd given the shot everything she had: a glistening décolletage, a generous glimpse of cleavage and more mascara than I think I've ever owned. She posed with head twisted coquettishly towards the camera over her right shoulder. It was all glamour and Hollywood, channelling the soaped-up, pouty allure of that Gina Lollobrigida scene in *Anna of Brooklyn*.

Only in this case, Anna was just twelve years old . . .

My daughter brought the photo to my attention. She was 'Oh, my *actual* God!' indignant; she *hated* the picture, called it for the attention-seeking crap that it was. To my relief, she was already someone who was never going to need that level of mass public approval and any one of her contemporaries who did met with her uncompromising disdain. And yet in spite of herself, and however genuine her dismissive scorn, my little girl was also suddenly overcome with emotion: flushed cheeks, damp eyes; voice catching in her throat.

I've frequently fallen victim to the same infuriating reflex response. Your head's busy serving up an honest, well-reasoned retort, while your subconscious shakes up a heady blend of hormone, phobia and unvoiced inadequacy. Before you know it, all of it's out there for everyone to see and there's nothing you can do but wait it out.

At her age and in this instance I would have reacted in *exactly* the same way. Even with my thirty-year advantage on her, I recall a similar guerrilla-assault on my composure the night a Chinese take-out with a bunch of mates ended in a spontaneous mass skinny dip in my mates' outdoor pool. It really *wasn't* something I felt the need to do; it wasn't a warm night, I wasn't feeling the lure of the water, and we were all forty-somethings in a suburban back garden, not on an 18–30s package holiday in Magaluf.

Besides, I knew my grey-whites would be the standout look of the night in the context of the co-ordinated lace sets my mates *happened* to be wearing. (One woman in particular had lingered over a lovely, slow reveal of scarlet lingerie; there was NOTHING spontaneous about this skinny-dip scenario . . .) So I knew *exactly* how that bath-time profile picture was affecting my daughter's equilibrium: a visceral aversion to any digital exhibitionism, muddied by the realisation that even had she felt so moved, she was way short of the required dose of *chutzpah*. That kind of self-knowledge is *crushing*: around the pool that night, I felt far from OK. I wasn't centred or grounded, or proud that I was able to function without audience approval; instead I felt a resurgence of a latent, adolescent fear: in comparison to my peers, I was devoid of allure, adventurousness. *Sex appeal.*

Christ, it's a horrible feeling!

Girl A has it, knows it; flaunts it. Girl B doesn't; hardly a new story. But what *is* new for our kids, *entirely* new, is that we had the luxury of being able to play out our bad decisions and poor judgements in real time, in the real world; generally they lasted a matter of moments and left more or less no trace, just memories, which, if you wait long enough, can be dismissed or owned, as the mood takes you. Similarly fleeting were the peer pressures that made moments of our adolescence intolerable.

In contrast, my daughter was immersed in a world where those same peer pressures confronted her and her mates 24/7. Anna may only have been flirting with her emerging womanhood from the alternative reality of a Lanzarote floating bar in the same way girls have done for generations from behind the privacy of a locked bathroom door. But thanks to smartphones, social media and a mother woefully unaware of her daughter's inadequate privacy settings, Anna's 'moment' will *remain* tangible. No doubt, it's still out there in the ether, God help her.

The irony was that her mother, a child psychologist, was noisily putting *space* and *privacy* at the heart of her approach to raising her daughter. The woman would no sooner read her daughter's Facebook page than she would her diary; we knew this, because she had made a point of telling us all – often. Which is all well and good, until your 12-year-old's flirty frolics find their way onto the phone of every pupil at the school, and who knows who else besides . . .

The ensuing furore represents a microcosm of everything that's shit for our kids about an adolescence played out under the relentless glare of social media. And it presented a labyrinthine set of problems for me too. First, there was the (brief) dilemma about the possible ramifications to my daughter's friendship with Anna, and mine with her mother, were I to interfere and make Anna's mother aware of how her particular 'privacy' policy was working out.

Second, social media and the pull of perfection is *insidious*. My daughter *knew* her intellectual response to Anna's big reveal was bang on – and I reinforced that message too, of course I did. At the same time, she was still just a gawky 13-year-old girl and that photo received in the region of 300 'likes'. There's an irrational, emotional 'safety' in such numbers for our kids. Those numbers, a peer-reviewed endorsement, *really matter* when you're twelve or thirteen: *you're in.*

Similarly, when that proportion of your peers add their little thumbs-up to a photograph, it's more than peer approval: it's a members list, a highly public declaration of membership. *I get this; I'm down with this.* So it's a big deal to dare to demonstrate your disapproval by refusing to *like* it. That matters – kids notice. Thanks to social media, this generation are not even permitted the luxury of keeping their *dissension* private. Their disapproval, or rather, their *lack* of approval, is marked up in a horribly public arena that takes no prisoners.

There's light at the end of this misery, however. Four or five years on, now aged seventeen, my daughter and her mates make social media work for them in a way that's frankly more sophisticated than most thirty/forty/fifty-somethings manage. One promotes her photography business on Facebook and Instagram, while another, an art student with a keen eye for everything vintage, has a successful small e-business selling vintage fashion. A bunch of her mates are in a band and use social media to post new tracks and to promote their latest gigs. Two enterprising young guys worked social media to fund a remarkable adventure to participate in a major disaster relief effort in the Philippines. More widely, my daughter's mates routinely use social media as a testing ground for their emerging humour, politics, cultural references and ethical debate. I see them using it as a debate club, a friendship network; a support group.

And Anna? I'm told she hasn't grown out of the need to post provocative selfies, nor of her desire to celebrate her voluptuous feminine allure. Good luck to her! I know plenty of forty-somethings still doing exactly that. But at least she's learned to secure her privacy settings.

> *Social media allows us to behave in ways that we are hardwired for in the first place – as humans.*
>
> *Francois Gossieaux*, The Hyper-Social Organization

SO . . .

♦ When it comes to living an e-life, our kids are pioneers, feeling their way through this stuff with very little help from clueless adulthood. This time, we really *haven't* been where they are and it's all too easy to underestimate the extent of the head-fuckery that comes with it.

♦ When your 10-year-old *BEGS* you to let them set up a Facebook account with a fake date of birth, resist . At that tender age, this stuff is *insidious;* there are *good* reasons why the minimum age is set at thirteen. Same time, staying clear until they're 'ready' is a tough call. Because when have teens *EVER* left off the adult stuff until adulthood? Weren't we always smoking/drinking/shagging before we were supposed to? Protect where we can, sanitise to a degree and then keep watching, keep talking, keep listening, keep modelling; wait it out.

♦ Once they're up and running with social media, *watch* their usage. Watch it really, really closely until you are confident that they're through the delicate, incendiary years. And all the while, model sensible usage. Be polite online. Always. Encourage them to challenge, to question, and to swim against the tide whenever it matters.

♦ It helps to remember that our kids are *not* living their social media lives in a vacuum – social networks are not separate and distinct from real life. The stability and security they get from you in the real world influences them *at every level*. Social media's no exception. Keep telling them, they'll get it. Five years on and seventeen years old and it's a new dawn: my daughter and her mates' online lives are a fabulous, exciting microcosm of life in the twenty-first century.

It's a whole. new. world. Even for those of us with a social media thing going on, we can have no idea what it feels like to be thirteen and immersed in all this. Take a look at YouTuber Todrick Hall (no, me either – I had to be steered in his direction by my 17-year-old). His colourful parody teen-heartache number, 'You Unfollowed Me' is pure genius and highlights some of the vicious e-comebacks posted online by the Dumped to their Dumpee.

Chapter 15

Privilege, a Dunking and Invisible Backpacks
Raising empathetic kids

AI

In 1988, Peggy McIntosh had one of those moments of clarity that changes everything. It was the sort of moment reserved for the great *thinkers* of our time. Like the glorious *tidiness* of Sir Tim Berners-Lee's nifty electronic filing system, initially hailed only by the science-types at CERN, now known universally as the World Wide Web. Or what was (probably) the single greatest humanitarian act of the twentieth century, the work of one Melitta Bentz of Germany, who in 1908, patented her divinely inspired filter coffee machine, thereby enabling generation upon generation of the Sleep-Deprived Masses to haul arse of a morning and *function*, thanks to a decent cup of coffee.

McIntosh and these others have a gift: while the rest of us blithely believe we know everything that matters about a thing, they open the door to a whole new way of seeing it. They change *everything*.

Peggy was an academic, a writer and feminist working in the USA when she realised that what was stopping her educated male colleagues coming to regard themselves as feminists was not that they didn't see the *sense* in equality, diversity or fairness. It was that they (we're talking educated white men) couldn't see themselves as inherently *privileged* in comparison to women. But she saw it, clear as day. She saw what she described as 'an invisible weightless knapsack of assurances, tools, maps, guides, codebooks, passports, visas, clothes, compass, emergency gear, and blank checks' carried by every single one of her male white colleagues. She knew too that Americans of colour would be seeing it just as sharply as she was.

This was already good stuff but the real *genius* of Peggy's idea was yet to come. Because if the men surrounding her at work couldn't see it, she pondered, what was it she herself wasn't seeing? What were the invisible contents of her own knapsack of privilege? What if she too, was blind to her own advantage?

The result was her groundbreaking essay, 'Unpacking the Invisible Knapsack', in which Peggy identified not those 'acts of meanness' carried out towards non-white Americans, but the less tangible stuff enjoyed without a second thought by white Americans everywhere. Being able to count on your neighbours being at worst 'neutral' towards you when you move to a new neighbourhood. Finding your culturally favourite foods well stocked on the shelves of your local Walmart. Being able to see newsreaders, law enforcers, politicians, who have the same skin colour as you.

Peggy realised that while she had devoted so much focus to her colleagues' knapsacks, the ones marked 'Male Privilege', she'd missed the fact that she had one of her own, marked, 'Caucasian'. And to her chagrin, she found it rammed full.

Great things are possible when you start trying to live your life through the lens of *'what do I have that others don't?'* Particularly when you start using your invisible toolkit on behalf of what's due – *especially* when you use it on behalf of what's due to others.

I'm reminded of the School Pool incident. My son would have been around twelve years old. It was winter: the pool was outdoors and therefore out of use, but on the day in question, it had been filled by maintenance folk after essential 'works'. When the pool-fixing folk headed off for a tea break, none of them noticed that the gate to the pool area had been left unlocked.

My son noticed. And so did a bunch of his mates from a younger year group. These lads, we called his 'Fan Club' and they *mattered* to my son: Down syndrome may have made it more tricky for him to keep up with their conversations, but it didn't make him any less keen on getting their attention. He'd do *anything* to get a laugh.

So I'm on the outside lane of the M4, halfway to London with a colleague when my phone rings: it's school. My colleague answers it for me.

My son, it seems, has wandered up to the poolside, carrying a younger lad in his arms, and thrown him in, fully clothed, at the deep end. As if this wasn't bad enough, he'd happened to pick on possibly the only kid in the school who still couldn't swim. I was assured that the lad was fine – shocked, but fine – but my son was in BIG trouble.

I was *mortified*. This was a new one, even for my boy. (Parents who don't have a learning-disabled child on roll at a mainstream school may not know the *terror* of serious misdemeanour: it carries with it an ever-present, low-level dread of imminent permanent exclusion.) He'd never done anything that might actually have endangered a life before. (OK, he could have had *no clue* the kid couldn't swim. And he had apparently quickly recognised he needed to help pull the lad out. And the gates *shouldn't* have been left open anyway. All the same, *really?*)

Obviously, learning disability or no, the school had to take action. I was *terrified*. But by the following day, two things had happened. The second of those was remarkable.

First, a sizeable tranche of the school's younger population found his actions nothing short of *heroic*. This had been an act of slapstick rebellion on a glorious scale and, unhelpfully, he was immediately pedestalised (they even set up a Facebook page in his name, declaring him 'A Legend'). The business of enlightening my lad of the error of his ways was made all the harder by the evident good health of the lad in question ('No harm done, eh, Mum?') and even *more* difficult by the fact that he was back-slapped, high-fived and lauded down every corridor.

But something else was happening. Quietly, a groundswell of action was taking place. The kids who knew my son best, the ones who had grown up with him from the age of four, were seeing this from a truly remarkable perspective. They were acting from one central premise: they were absolutely confident of his lack of ill intent.

A core of these fabulous kids developed the conviction that he would never have had the idea for these shenanigans himself; someone else had put him up to it. And they began to advocate to the teaching staff on his behalf. They insisted on his good nature, cited previous lesser incidents of incitement and demanded that staff look beyond the incident to identify the *agents provocateurs*.

Initially, the teachers asked my son outright, but at the age of twelve he wasn't yet clearly able to recount events in any useful order. But in any case, in this instance, he didn't need to: his mates were on it. CCTV, they insisted, would tell all. His learning support assistant was impressed and got on the case. After ploughing through hours of tape, sure enough, there it was: a little band of troopers, caught on film, lurking at the edges of the pool. Lads who knew enough not to step into the pool area, but not enough to discourage my boy from doing so.

The beauty of an education that embraces diversity: in the years they had got to know him, my lad's mates had steadily learned to unpack their own backpack. They embraced without question a reciprocal friendship with a lad with everything to give but with what they could clearly see was a less well-stocked toolkit. And there they were, finding the confidence to stand up for what was due to him when they saw it lacking.

My God, their parents should be proud – those kids were *brilliant*! And their actions spoke volumes to those younger lads who learned, just by watching, how they *should* have played it. And that actually, it *is* cool to stand up for fairness, to do right by folk. Publicly.

Peggy's essay wasn't just a truly creative academic exercise, it was a call to arms. It held a mirror up to everyone who previously believed themselves fair and decent and challenged us all not just to focus on those things that are stacked against us, but to unpack our own privileges, see ourselves in full context.

To truly embrace diversity, we have to first acknowledge the power and freedoms stashed away in our backpacks and then to rage on behalf of those without those same privileges. This, it seems to me, needs to be at the heart of modern feminism: it demands we stand up for what's due, to *anyone*, regardless, but that we start from a place of real integrity, a little humility and a whole lot of empathy. And surely that's a job description no parent would reject.

(My son, if you're wondering, actually *is* a legend, though not because he chucked a non-swimmer, fully clothed, into the school pool. He wrote a letter of apology, had a stern talking-to and briefly feigned a penitent ambition to work as a lifeguard. I've no idea whether the experience finally persuaded the other lad to learn to swim, but I hope so – silver linings and all that.)

> *We're all put ahead and behind by the circumstances of our birth. We all have a combination of both. And it changes minute by minute, depending on where we are, who we're seeing, or what we're required to do.*
>
> Peggy McIntosh, in an interview for *The New Yorker*, May 2014

> *Nobody can give you equality or justice or anything . . . you take it.*
>
> Malcolm X

SO . . .

♦ This is all about empathy – the ability to confidently name a wide range of emotions when you are experiencing them yourself and when you see them in the face of others around you. Research suggests that the empathetic child does better: makes better decisions that are to their own benefit but that don't impact negatively on the feelings of others. More resilient, they are better equipped to withstand bullying, peer pressure and setbacks. And they tend to fare better academically. But mainly, empaths are just *nicer*. They're good to be around, good to work with and good to live with.

♦ The key message here is the same old thing: model it. We have to *be* empathetic and compassionate in order to raise empathetic kids. Course, there's stuff we can *do* to encourage our kids, but *no amount of talking the talk* is going to help build empathy and compassion in our kids unless they *see* bucketfuls of it in our interactions with them and with other people, every day. So model it.

♦ It starts on Day One. Empathetic parents work hard to respond to their infant's emotional needs. The child who is comforted when in pain, reassured when nervous, enabled when hesitant, will feel like their emotions *matter*. That means that they are more likely to grow up seeing the emotions of others around them matter too. It makes sense.

◆ As your kids grow, be patient when someone makes a mistake in your presence. Talk about how it *feels* to be the person getting it wrong; be compassionate. Then ask your kids to join in the conversation about it. Name it, when your kids show compassion and praise it – 'Oh, that's *such* a kind way to look at it. You're right: he *must* have felt bad/silly/worried then, yes.'

◆ We aren't always nice – well, we aren't. There will always be times when we kick off when we're tired and up against it, and someone throws something new and *exhausting* into the mix. Some of those times will be happening right in front of our kids. But that's OK: what matters is *not* that we're perfect, compassionate, empathetic creatures at every turn but that when we mess up, we apologise, in front of the kids. We're none of us perfect but that's OK: we're good enough. When we get it wrong, it's not about what we *do*, it's about what we do *next*. So call the moment for what it was: *That wasn't fair of me. I was tired, and I took it out on Mummy/Daddy/Grandma/the slow fella in front of us in the queue. I'm sorry – that must have made you all feel really unhappy.*

◆ Compliment folk, including your kids, lots. Not the superficial stuff – *Wow, that outfit looks great on you!* – but the stuff that lingers, the stuff that helps build you a grown-up – *You moved out of the way on the bus so that that lady could get past you. That was so thoughtful.* Or how about, *I am so happy that you shared your snack with your friend at the park today. Do you think she was feeling a bit sad because you had one and she didn't?*

◆ At the same time, don't go crazy with the compliments – it dilutes the impact if you're praising their every move. Besides, it gets weird.

♦ Say things like, 'I know you're feeling really cross because you really want to play with that toy right now, but it isn't OK to throw things.' Don't say, 'That's naughty.'

♦ Say things like, 'I know you're feeling upset at your brother for snatching your snack from you, but how do you think he feels now that you've hit him?' Don't say, 'That's naughty.'

♦ Say things like, 'What can you do to make your brother feel better?' Don't just say, 'Say sorry.'

♦ There's a lot to be said for taking time to build your child's emotional vocabulary. Emotions are *complicated*, so why leave it to chance? Why assume that somewhere between the ages of one and twenty-one, they'll figure it all out by social osmosis? No, tackle this stuff *head on*. Keep emotions on the agenda, a little and often. Try some of this:

Sit with your pre-schooler and your primary school-aged kids, look for faces in magazines and cut out emotional expressions. Make a feelings board.

At story time, talk about how the actions of the characters made the others *feel*. Name the emotions. Bring in your feelings board and get them to match it all up.

As the kids get older, have similar chats about emotionally affecting plot lines of movies, telly and books.

When they talk through teen traumas, speculate together about the driving emotions of any wrongdoer. Get them to see a problem from the other person's perspective and then talk about whether that changes anything.

> *Seek first to understand, then to be understood.*
>
> *Stephen R. Covey*, Seven Habits of Highly Effective People

Alanis Morissette's 'Empathy' is an ode to empaths everywhere, to those beautiful folk who make the lonely and invisible feel noticed and understood. And it's the perfect, blissful choice to play right now. Because that's it, isn't it? That's the people we want our people to be. Beautiful!

Chapter 16

The Flasher Down the Lane: Memories of Childhood Vulnerability
Raising safe, independent kids

Al

Of all my girlfriends when I was a kid, my mate Beccy was the most sassy. I can leaf through the full catalogue of moments in my childhood where I put myself at my most vulnerable and in almost every case, Beccy was just out of shot, fearlessly leading the way in braided pigtails, battered espadrilles and her mother's old bottle-green crocheted mini dress. (I say 'old': it was a sixties original and today would come with a hefty price tag in some chic vintage boutique. Back in 1982, however, it was the kind of thing dug out of the back of your mother's wardrobe. Becs' mother's dress was eye-wateringly short, definitely not *de rigueur* for 1982 Brum; Becs therefore wore it constantly, with knickerless, gleeful defiance.)

She was fabulous, but I wince at the risks we took – the injuries, incidents, accidents and tragedies that could so easily have happened.

The many, many times when no one, not a single soul, knew where we were.

'We'll be fine, I was a Girl Guide,' Becs would trot out, confidently. 'I've always got 2p for the phone box.' Bostin!

Adult-me struggles to reconcile the risks with the undeniable *bliss* of those unfettered adventures with Becs, gashed knees and close calls notwithstanding. Without doubt those were formative experiences, which shaped the adult I was about to become. I was a risk-averse child, always three steps ahead of myself, assessing every possible repercussion and generally concluding, 'Best not.'

At Becs' insistence, I acquiesced in plans that took me way out of my comfort zone. Like the times we took the short cut home after late-night drama rehearsals, taking us on a perilously unpopulated and unlit route along the canal path, torchless on pitch-black winter nights. Then there was the summer afternoon when we wandered through a field of barley at the end of my road and stumbled upon an adulterous copulation between a bloke from across the road and a fabulously top-heavy blonde. (She straddled him, wearing nothing but the indelible stain of her mortal sin. Becs and I were thirteen and from Catholic school: I was all for running the hell away, certain something Satanic was happening. To my horror, Becs was *fascinated* and insisted we stay, crawling commando-style through the barley for a better look.)

Inevitably, some of Becs' rampant passion for a life filled with experience started to rub off. I grew more curious, more interested, sought more answers. In 1981, 14-year-old me found myself stepping off a National Express coach to march alongside Becs on the streets of London, waving 'Ban the Bomb' and 'Fall Out With Thatcher' banners. We linked arms in the face of a row of mounted police in Hyde Park and listened wide-eyed as Tony Benn showed us for the first time that politics didn't have to be all Thatcherite miner-bashing and faux humility.

I started to learn that maybe I could try life on my own terms; I could dip my toe into what life had to offer; that maybe it would be OK. As I watched Becs, I yearned for a little of her audacious sense of entitlement to life and copied her as much as I dared. I started to get braver, all on my own.

My emerging courage was timely: walking home late one cold night, I dared myself to take a risk: the short cut home, all on my own. I had braved it with Becs, hadn't I? No harm done. It would be fine.

One section of the short cut took me down a narrow, ill-lit alley, fenced in on both sides. It ran for about a half-mile and turned forty-five-degree angles three times. In places, the upright posts of the fence had broken away, leaving gaping holes where brambles made a bid for freedom.

My heart raced at every corner and more so each time I approached sections of broken fence: these felt exposed, unquantifiable. But, channelling Becs as hard as I could, I pushed on, daring myself not to break into a run. At last, I passed the last of the gaps, a couple of hundred yards from the end of the alleyway, and exhaled a little.

And that's when he called to me.

'Hey!'

He had appeared at the edge of the last of the gaps in the fence, his left hand gripping the higher of two horizontal posts, his face masked by a large bandana. Initially, I was more confused than scared: what was he doing and what was *with* that mask? He looked *ridiculous*.

Having turned to face him, I realised I had taken a step towards him.

'Come here, that's right,' he said, faking an Irish accent really badly.

I almost laughed. And then my eyes scanned down the length of him and I realised his right hand was pumping away at his penis, just above the lower of the two horizontal posts. I froze, struggling to process the disconnect of all these bizarre, disparate pieces of information.

At last, adrenalin kicked in.

'You sick bastard!' I called and ran like hell, my hand reaching into my pocket for my emergency 2p, my sights set on the phone box at the end of the road.

I had faced the biggest risk of my life to date, and faced it alone.

My parents reported the flasher down the lane to the police, who patrolled the area for a while. He wasn't seen again. I had been given enough independence by my parents to experience my little corner of the world on my own terms. Their trust (in me? in society? in the ultimate OK-ness of everything?) had enabled me to explore the world through Becs' eyes; she in turn had stamped some spontaneity on my life, in a way no amount of parenting could have done. Nestled under her uninhibited wing, I learned to exhale a little – to trust that all would (probably) be OK. And to always carry a two-pence piece, just in case it actually wasn't.

Reflecting back on that time in my life is hard now, as a parent. Because Adult-me is back to full-on risk-analysis, only this time I'm doing it on behalf of my kids. I'm way ahead of their every step, seeing broken glass and paedos behind every broken fence panel. Letting them loose, as it turns out, is really, really hard.

But my pensive, risk-averse daughter *needs* a Becs in her life, and she needs to be given the freedom to learn about life on her own terms, same as I did; I know that. There are days when life seems to be filled with more peril than ever before, and I'm almost overwhelmed by the urge to strap the kids to a fifty-metre tether on the front lawn. But I fight it. Instead I affect a nonchalant tone and say, 'OK, have fun' and I watch my daughter go, taking a little comfort that where I had an emergency 2p in my pocket, she has Apple. Modernity isn't all bad and thank the Great Lord Jobs in the Sky for that.

> *Think for a minute, darling: in fairy tales it's always the children who have the fine adventures. The mothers have to stay at home and wait for the children to fly in the window.*
>
> *Audrey Niffenegger,* The Time Traveler's Wife

SO . . .

The honest truth is there are vast sections of those early years with your kids when it's a daily battle *not* to overprotect. Risk is *everywhere* and if you give in to the fear, you'll be sanitising their young lives to the brink of lunacy before you know it.

Breathe, take a moment. Fill that moment with the deliciously soothing sounds of Sia's 'Lullaby'. She'll relax those shoulders and remind you that life is all about 'doing the work' and trusting it'll work out well in the end. She gets, too, that along the way there will always be falls, knocks and setbacks – we just have to pick ourselves up and get back on it. We know this already, but sooner or later, we have to let our kids find it out for themselves too. If, unfathomably, Sia's not enough, pour yourself a gin too – we need you calm for this next bit . . .

♦ We have to ease up just enough to give our kids the sense of freedom they need to thrive. We're not saying that's easy: it's not. It's really tough, but there are things you can do to make it easier. Top of the list: skill them up.

♦ We need kids that have a sound grasp of their personal space, and of their right for that to be respected. Kids who understand their right to privacy and who are enabled to make real choices and gain a sense of control over their lives. Because kids like this are likely to develop a robust self-esteem. And that goes a really long way towards getting them to the point where they are confident enough to take *controlled* risks, but also to speak up when things aren't right.

♦ Public and Private: Make sure your children have a working understanding of the concepts of 'public' and 'private' from an early age. If you know that they get that 'private' is when they're alone in the bathroom and no one can see them, for instance, you'll know they can reliably express themselves if that privacy is challenged. In time, that understanding can be extended to which parts of their body are private and which are public, and that's an empowering thing to know about yourself.

♦ Self-expression: Revisit some of that work from Chapters 4 and 6 on respecting personal space, not sweating the small stuff and making sure your kids taste real choice and genuine control over enough aspects of their lives. Make absolutely certain that your desire to ensure they are safe and healthy at all times isn't stifling them. They *have* to be able to express their personalities and that means that we as adults must respect their tastes, within reason, in clothes, food and friends.

♦ Circles of Familiarity: This is a simple visual teaching aid often used for children with learning disabilities, but it's one we can all learn from. The idea is to have a picture that is a series of differently coloured concentric circles, as in archery. At the centre, in the bull's-eye, place a picture of your child (or get them to draw themselves) and then alongside that the names/photos of those closest to them – parents, best friend and so on. You then place other people in their life in the circles moving outwards to show the varying levels of connection, right up to strangers on the outside of all the circles. In doing this process you talk about different types of touch and conversation. Who it is OK to have special hugs with, who it isn't, and what sort of things we talk about with the different people in our lives. It's all fluid – changing as the child grows, people come and go, and the landscape of their world alters.

♦ Try it about yourself and the people in your life first. And then get your child to think about who s/he would add to their own set of circles. Get them to think about who has their trust and gets to stand appropriately close and what touch and chat looks like in all their other relationships, children and grown-ups alike. This exercise also helps them to understand about the personal space of others, building their social dexterity from a strong sense of knowing boundaries and enjoying happy, healthy interactions. It can be incredibly powerful.

♦ Privacy: As our children grow, they start to develop an intrinsic need for privacy. As adolescence looms, there's one message you have to come to terms with: *you are no longer going to be able to know everything about your child.* It can't be done and what's more, it probably *shouldn't* be done. Give them the security of knowing that their space is their space; a place to retreat, where they can figure out a few things and emerge a little clearer-headed. Or else emerge when they're ready to ask for help, to seek clarity from you.

♦ Don't pry: don't read diaries, messenger or texts. In any case their written words here represent only a fleeting *moment* of where their head's at. During the turbulent teen years, their heads will be in a million different places, changing constantly. Reading a snapshot of that in black and white will do you no good. So respect their privacy, let them know you're present, calm and listening. And *don't* freak at revelations when they are offered up; thank them for their honesty.

Listen. It's hard, granted, but trust us, it's the best way to *properly* get to know what's going on in their lives.

♦ Honestly, these are *huge* lessons, about what's acceptable in relationships, what's OK in any one interaction with another human, and what really isn't. Where better and safer to learn some of those rules than in their early interactions with you?

> *It is the nightly custom of every good mother after her children are asleep to rummage in their minds and put things straight for next morning. When you wake in the morning, the naughtiness and evil passions with which you went to bed have been folded up small and placed at the bottom of your mind; and on the top, beautifully aired, are spread out your prettier thoughts, ready for you to put on.*
>
> J. M. Barrie, Peter Pan

'Not Asking for it' – Tuesday afternoon in ASDAN

Vik

Channel 4's fly-on-the-wall *Educating Essex/Cardiff/Yorkshire* has given splendid insight into secondary schools and their students and staff. Here's some more real classroom life, the stuff parents would *LOVE* to eavesdrop on . . .

> *It's raining and we are in a temporary classroom, my colleague Matt (Mr D) and our Year 10 ASDAN group (Life Skills) and me. It's the last period of the day. We are supposed to be finishing a traffic survey and writing up the costing of a package holiday but somehow that has segued into talk of last Friday's events at the Youth Club.*

> *I have coffee, fig rolls, and no desire to stop the flow of chat in pursuit of a curricular objective. And well, this happened . . .*
>
> The Students: Ellie, George, Jordan, Lauren and Legolas (yes, *Legolas*)

Ellie: Sir, can we watch *American Pie*? It's nearly half term.

Mr D: Ellie, it's January the *ELEVENTH*.

George: It's educational, though.

Mr D: This I have to hear – in what way is it educational, George?

George: It's about learning about your body: Sex Education, pretty much PSHE [Personal, Social and Health Education]. Except entertaining and not like when Miss Taylor does it for us and just makes us do a wordsearch about chlamydia.

Lauren: I'm so not watchin' that! It's got them sticking their bits in fruit, that's totally disgusting.

Ellie: Shut up, is it?

George: He's experimenting, the kid, that's all. Someone tells him that when you do it, it feels all warm, like an apple pie. My brother says it's hilarious because his dad catches him but then tries to be all cool about it.

Mr D: I can't imagine my father having been cool about that. But then I can't say I ever thought about baked goods in that way . . .

Jordan: They had it on at Youth House last Friday.

Lauren: What, apple pie?

Jordan: No, *American Pie*, you dick!

Me: Don't say dick, Jordan.

Lauren: I don't think girls would like it much. I bet it's all about the boys trying to shag all the girls and that.

Ellie: It's s'posed to be proper funny, though, Lar.

Jordan: I didn't see all of it. Jack Walsh got into a fight with Lee Cleeves.

Ellie: Was it about Laura Miles?

Jordan: Yeah, annoying bitch.

Ellie: Um, actually, Jordan, she's not . . .? Lee Cleeves is a massive dick. Sorry, Miss.

George: He thinks he's *GOT* a massive dick, ha! Sorry, Miss.

Me: Appreciated, people. I know Lee, what happened?

Ellie: You best not know, Miss, because then it'll get all teachery and like, I can't be arsed with that, but to be fair, none of the workers at Youth House had a clue what went on.

Me: So, I think you're going to have to tell me now, Ellie – I am hugely intrigued.

George: Are we watching *American Pie* then?

Mr D: Unlikely, George. I'd get my P45.

George: What's that?

Mr D: It's a piece of paper from the Head, saying, 'You can't be a teacher any more because you let 15-year-olds watch sex on the telly in school.'

George: Mrs Dee would be well pissed then, eh?

Mr D: Mrs Dee would, as you say, George, 'be well pissed' – she does like a nice paid mortgage.

Me: Ellie, is Laura your friend?

Lauren: No, she was that girl that moved to Headwell. We did all go around with her when she was here, but then she left halfway through Year 9.

Ellie: She was a bit stuck-up, but I quite liked her. She comes up to Youth House though now. She didn't really make any, like, friends and stuff at Headwell.

Jordan: She used to be stuck-up but now she's a slag.

Me: I have a real problem with that word, Jordan.

Jordan: Yeah, but we all know what it means.

Lauren: You think you know what it means but you never ever say it about boys and that pisses me right off. Lee Cleeves is a massive slag.

Jordan: Yeah, but Laura is a *proper* slag. She comes up Youth House and she makes out she's it. She was leant over the pool table and we could all see her G-rope.

Ellie: All right, but still.

Lauren: Yeah, because you all look at her and she laps it up – it makes her worse.

Me: Why did Jack and Lee fight?

Mr D: Yes, I'm finding I need the backstory now.

Jordan: Laura was going out with Jack but she got off with Lee and it all just kicked off.

Ellie: That's not what I heard.

Lauren: No, nor me.

Me: What did you hear?

Ellie: Laura and Jack shagged. And when Lee found out, he thought they would shag too. So they went to her sister's to babysit and they had loads of cider and stuff and he was pushing her. She said she didn't want to, though.

Me: Are you saying he raped her?

Lauren: No, they didn't have sex, Miss – not in the end. But he was proper vile to her about it and when Jack found out, he had a massive go at Lee. Which was fair play, to be fair.

George: Can we watch Friends then, Sir?

Mr D: Shut up, George. Plan your week in Majorca.

Me: Jordan, so why is Laura a slag then? Why describe her as that?

Ellie: Because he's too thick to come up with proper words.

Jordan: She was asking for it and so Lee thought it was going to happen and then she's all like, 'No, I don't want that now.'

Lauren: Yes, exactly Jordan, she said *NO*.

Jordan: But she's a prick tease.

Ellie: I know what you are saying, but it don't matter. And if they were both pissed then that is mad.

Me: Jordan, what does 'asking for it' mean?

Jordan: Oh, Miss, this is getting out of hand now. I'm doing my traffic survey.

Lauren: No way, Jordan! You can't go around saying words like 'slag' and things like 'asking for it' and not expect people to be annoyed. Miss is not exactly going to let you get away with that, is she?

Mr D: Jordan, what does 'asking for it' mean?

Jordan: Sir, you know.

Mr D: I think we all know that I know an enormous amount, Jordan – you've been in my history class. But I'm curious. What is 'it' and how exactly was Laura doing the requesting?

Jordan: What?

Mr D: OK. George, what does 'asking for it' mean?

George: What?

Mr D: I need fig rolls.

Ellie: Jordan, you mean that if a girl dresses in, like, short skirts and that and flirts, she is asking for someone to try and shag her, don't you?

Jordan: Well, yeah. I mean I'm not saying that she's asking to be raped, I'm saying that she's like, saying to boys, 'I'm up for it.'

Me: Do any of you think it was OK for Lee to be annoyed when Laura said she didn't want to have sex?

George: It's not OK for him to push her around but I can see he would be pissed off.

Ellie: Yeah, all right, but it's one thing to be pissed off that something didn't happen that you wanted to happen, but just because she had a mini dress on and wants a boyfriend a bit too much, it's like, that doesn't mean pricks like Lee can just do and say what they want about her. It doesn't mean pricks like you can say what they want either, Jordan. I think she's really lonely at her school and she's just getting it a bit wrong when she comes back round here.

Me: Ellie, I think what you said is really spot-on. Jordan, what d'ya say to that?

Jordan: I get that, but still . . .

Lauren: Still *what*, Jord?

Jordan: It's like controlling yourself and that.

Mr D: Jordan, I taught you about evolution in Year 8. I don't expect you to remember a great deal about that, despite my excellent teaching, but remember this: you have this thing in your trousers you are currently thrilled about and you are keen to test its wonders. As a ridiculously handsome man, I understand this. But we have evolved, us humans, to have these incredible brains that enable us to control our animal urges: it allows us to keep our dicks in check and not *BE* dicks. Sorry, Miss!

Me: Get out of my classroom.

Jordan: All right, yeah, I get that. To be fair, Lee *is* a dick!

George: Sir, can we watch *The Full Monty* then, please?

Mr D: George, a foray into the impact of *Thatcher's Britain* would be a huge treat and I don't blame you for asking so nicely but I think what we have learned this afternoon is no means no. No?

Legolas: Miss, can I go to my lute class now, please?

Chapter 17

Toast, Hot Chocolate and Love: On Teens, on a Train, on a Journey to Sexuality Central
Raising kids with self-worth

Vik

It's the Millennium. And I am working at a local secondary school in the Learning Support Team. Increasingly, in our mouldy but cosy clutch of rooms, we found ourselves mopping up the kids who, for a huge variety of reasons, couldn't cope with the emotional and academic demands of school life. We knew their stories, we knew their parents, and we were working out how to keep them together and keep them out of the eyeline of the colleagues who had been told to 'Piss off' almost hourly by one or two of their number.

I was massively blessed to work under the direction of a SENCO (Special Needs Coordinator), who had a deep dislike of the doctrines of testing and league tables and a lifelong and loud commitment to kids who were fragile. Even the 6 ft 2 in pierced 15-year-old dudes who would tower over her in a dyslexia/testosterone-fuelled rage. Especially them. She was 5 ft 2 in, a Quaker – an absolute powerhouse. The kids adored her; I adored her. She taught me to go with my instinct and along with my warm and talented colleagues she drove a philosophy that enabled us to reach out and lean in to the kids that needed us most. Our strategy wouldn't impress OFSTED or look good on a mission statement or prospectus. It wasn't 'Aspire, motivate, achieve', it was more 'Come in, be safe, have some toast'.

We wanted to take our 'love and hot chocolate' crew to the Dome for the exhibition that would last for just that year. Senior managers were sceptical about our young people's ability to be there without burning things down but SENCO Jan was having none of it and before we knew it, we were in Greenwich with eight of our alumni. As we walked towards this enormous sphere, one of our 'special' twins, Lee, turned to his brother Ryan and said, 'This is going to be TOTAL shit!' We weren't in *ANY WAY* nervous, us staff.

It was one of the best days of my career. All it needed was a Richard Curtis-styley soundtrack. The kids were interested, lit up and relaxed. Free from the conveyor-belt routine of school and the constant demand to achieve, they rocked up like Ribena-powered 5-year-olds to exhibits and activities they would usually have deemed 'lame' or 'gay'. They gave their reputations a rest . . .

So we're on the train, clunking home, knackered but happy. We've allowed the kids space to roam a bit, but most are sat snoozily, looking out windows or casually whacking each other with the sleeves of their sweatshirts. One of them, Mia, comes and finds me, taking the empty seat by my side.

'Miss?'

'Yes, love,' I answer.

'This has been the best day of my life,' she replies and rests her head on my arm, looking down the carriage.

I swallow down the tears. This girl has a heartbreakingly broken family. She is bright, hauntingly beautiful, but almost entirely disaffected by school and authority. In class, she is either missing entirely or when present, hugely disruptive or totally silent, picking at her bloodied filthy nails.

'Oh, Mia!' I say, hugging her, 'I am so, *so* pleased you liked it. You've been amazing company all day.'

Her expression is sad, unchanged, and then she tells me: 'I just gave Kris Lewis a blow job in the toilets.'

This is one of the standout *lines* of my career: 'So, where you gonna take *THAT* bad boy then, Miss?'

Me: 'Mia, darlin', *WHY?*'

Mia: 'He might like me.'

Soon, we disembark and debrief as the kids disperse. Home, and I head upstairs to where my daughter, aged six, sleeps blissfully. I look at her and feel an overwhelming surge of relief. She will *NEVER* experience so little self-worth; she will *NEVER* use sex as a way to be liked. She's safe; her life is not like Mia's.

But here's the thing: I couldn't know that for sure. Adored, nurtured children arrive into adolescence feeling and experiencing every shade and hue of the spectrum of identity. They fall prey to a culture that uses sex to sell yoghurt, for Christ's sake. They are, now, the multi-filtered Instagram generation. Most won't casually fellate on public transport but it doesn't mean they won't make crappy moves because they ache to feel attractive and longed for.

Right then my baby girl was a way off this chapter, but the girls, the rapidly rising young women that I was working with every day, they were calling out and calling us to arms. I had so much to learn.

Me: Mia, I totally get why you did what you just did. It's been a really weird and special day and those kinda days can make us behave in ways we wouldn't normally. Kris is good-looking and funny, and I bet he will be chuffed about what just happened. But I think he will remember more this morning when you climbed up into the Body in the Dome and you were laughing together and I noticed what you did then: I saw you read the words at the bottom to him because you know he struggles. He let you do it, which is huge for him and he was dead grateful. And you had a laugh. And see that, right: there was *ENOUGH* for him to think you're amazing – because you are.

With a little time and a lot of love, our kids will figure out that they are a person worth knowing. Until they get there, take comfort in Crowded House's gentle anthem to anyone who's ever stared in a mirror and struggled to see just how lovely they truly are: 'You're Not The Girl You Think You Are'. You're a whole lot lovelier!

SO . . .

♦ This, perhaps more than any other aspect of parenting, can be personally very difficult. Not just because of our wider fears around sexuality for our growing kids, but because of our own experiences. They can painfully colour how we even get started here. Be kind to yourself but recognise that those fears can translate into insightful, warm and supportive conversations with our kids when we take time to think about their importance and how we create space for them in our homes.

♦ The notion that girls and women are no longer subject to a stream of sexual comment that is very often abusive is frankly, bollocks! Laura Bates' Everyday Sexism project has revealed the truth, peppering Twitter feeds daily with examples of how even walking down the street can be crushing, terrifying or at best, a wearisome experience for anyone who happens to be female.

♦ Raising girls who feel comfortable in their own skin and can summon robust challenges to these scenarios is vital. Raising boys who not only would never dream of calling out something lewd to a passing girl but would also challenge the laddism that keeps it alive is just as vital.

♦ Who we *are* is, as ever, huge in this aspect of our parenting. Our kids need to see and feel appreciation of femininity and masculinity, a comfortable and individual ease in the expression of that in *us*, our natural mammalian urges embraced. They also need to hear our challenge to the sexist and damaging culture they are observing around them.

♦ So, when watching music or movies, let out equally raucous 'phwoars' for Benedict Cumberbatch and Beyoncé. They are extraordinary, brilliant and gorgeous, come *on*! But have Mum *and* Dad throw things at the telly in response to lazy and damaging depictions of woman as perma half-naked, screechy and powerless. Pour deep scorn on the scripts and images that show men as perma hard, emotionally remote and absolutely always the President of the United States. As a family, enjoy massive fandom for the actors, characters and writers in our culture that turn all that crap on its head while still giving us delicious and exciting light and shade in our drama.

♦ How do other adults around them behave? I have some truly lovely men in my wider family circle but Jesus, the misogyny moments we've endured! One older male relative, indignant, looking *me* straight in the eye on telling a tale about his son's workplace angst: 'And *NOW* they have put a *WOMAN* in there! Can you believe that?' Even when my husband quickly pointed out his glaringly offensive error, there wasn't a huge tremor in his diatribe, but our son on hearing his dad's words? Priceless. Another of the uncles has a habit of reducing every woman he knows to the size of her breasts: my husband's visible eye roll and refusal to join in? Doubly priceless.

♦ Our sexuality encompasses so much of what we are; how we think of ourselves, how we relate to others. There is nowhere NEAR enough attention paid to this in schools, when as I write the SRE (Sexuality & Relationships Education) curriculum is still not compulsory. Campaign for it in your child's secondary school. Young people need this taught properly, with educators who feel confident enough to create an environment where identity, gender stereotyping, rape, self-worth and being LGBT (Lesbian, Gay, Bisexual and Transgender) – all of these vital issues – are given the time, space and importance that they need. It trumps getting thirteen GCSEs at A* every time.

♦ We need to change the narrative around young people at home and in school to equip them for a happy and healthy emotional life: young adults who can respectfully enjoy their own and each other's bodies without feeling shame and without hurting either themselves or others. Make a choice early on that these things matter more to you than academic success. Real success is about relationships. Say that out loud – and keep saying it.

Chapter 18

A Saturday Night, Suburbia, c. 2004
Raising the topic of porn

Vik

Dear Kids

Have a great time with Nan tonight. Don't make her watch Paranormal Activity – *remember the open-heart surgery she's had. Also, don't let her have a fourth gin. It might seem funny in the moment but she will reveal stuff about her life with her first husband that will scar you. Trust Mummy on this one.*

Not that she isn't full of wisdom about life and relationships, of course. I know that even when she's going on and on (and you are tuning out), you're dead impressed with the life she's led. I cringe of course but I know you think she's cool – which she is: inappropriate, but cool.

There's stuff that Nan helped me to understand about boyfriends and girlfriends that I want you to know too but when I try to bring it up, you sometimes give me that face that makes me feel like I'm the mum in Meet The Fockers. *I am actually a bit flattered you think I look like Barbra Streisand in a kaftan and I LOVE that character, but I'm trying to be cool and not be too free and easy on the 'sex chat'. I know you would rather I embarrassed just a little easier than I do.*

Here's the thing, babies. You are at the point in your life where you have a million questions about love and sex and all of it. I know you don't want the answers from us face to face. Mostly. Chances are we won't have them anyway and actually, all of what you need to know will reveal itself as you meet people, fall in and out of love maybe, and work out what YOUR answers are for YOUR life. Before that gets under way, here's some ideas though to send you on your way.

Humour me. Read them. OK?

1. *Sex doesn't look like it does on the internet. Not unless the porn you may have stumbled upon (don't lie) is really unusual in that it features real people who (a) lean on each other's hair at the wrong moment, (b) apologise for a lot of what they are doing and (c) really like each other.*

2. *In real life, sex doesn't generally last for hours and involve really uncomfortable shoes. At its best, it's kinder, lovelier, more fun and to be honest, quicker.*

3. *This next sentence might be troubling but stay with me, kids. If Mummy made porn, I would do it all differently. It's dead exciting and completely natural to want to watch sex. For men AND women. But a lot of women don't like porn because the women in the films are often treated badly. It's unhelpful for young men too because they then think 'Christ, I've got to keep a stiffy for like, HOURS, and do at*

least seven positions. I would be happy with just a look at this point'. Bad porn (most porn) makes young people think sex is mildly/heavily abusive towards women, involves really uncomfortable-looking sofas and bodies that are entirely hair-free.

4. *You are learning about safety. That's so important. Keep that message with you always. Have fun but look after your body. But safety is more than just protection and STIs and all the stuff you'll do loads of in school. It's about taking care of your identity and your self-respect. Not every sexual encounter will be about being in love with that person necessarily; I get that. That's OK as long as you love yourself ALWAYS. Never, ever – promise me – be in a situation that doesn't feel good, respectful, equal or fun. If it doesn't feel right or safe, it probably isn't, so just bale. Sex can make you find things out about yourself that are simply magical because when it's good, it's amazing; it's the BEST. Sometimes though it's just OK, and a bit boring. Sometimes it's disappointing. Be kind, talk to and listen to the other person; understand that you are both filled with all sorts of worries about this stuff and no one rocks up into their sexual world with a set of skills and moves, ready to roll.*

5. *WOMEN LOVE SEX JUST AS MUCH AS MEN AND THEY LIKE TALKING ABOUT IT TOO. THIS MAKES THEM NORMAL, NOT SLUTS. THE RULES ARE THE SAME. CHALLENGE ANYONE WHO SUGGESTS OTHERWISE. IT'S NOT THE BLOODY 1950S!*

Nan never sat me down and talked to me or your aunties and uncle about sex. Parents mostly didn't do anything like that back then. But she talked about life and love. We saw her and Grandad hug and kiss, and heard them laughing in their room. I'll be honest, I could have done without the snoggin' in the kitchen while she had the mushy peas on but I expect you feel the same way about me and Dad of a Friday when we're excited about Chilli Night.

If she does have that gin later, she might say, 'You know it's nice to be important, but it's important to be nice.' That was something my dad always used to say. It's totally right. Be nice to yourself, and to other people. It's really no more complicated than that in terms of all you need to know about men and women and relationships. Honestly.

I'm going to shut up now and get me kaftan on because I'm super-keen to get Daddy out for that curry. We love you guys but it'll be good to get away from your need for learning for a bit. Knackered, we are. Does that make me sound like Yoda?

Oh, there's Magnums in the freezer.

Love

Mum x

Musical interlude, don't you think? Can't think of a more perfect lyric for a moment like this than Prefab Sprout's 'Billy', Paddy McAloon's gorgeous celebration of little boys letting their feelings show while practising 'long and slow' on their trumpets . . .

Chapter 19

The Irrepressible, Rebellious Teenager: 'Twas Ever Thus
Raising kids who respect the rules but know when to break them

Al

The teenager . . . A confession: I thought I could *predict* what the flashpoint would be, where it would come. I could pre-empt it, sidestep it with perfect parenting. I would be alert to it; sensitive, supportive. I would find the *perfect* phrase, settle nerves, allay trepidation . . . Fix it . . . Gently, quietly. There wouldn't be a raised voice or a slammed door.

But I was mistaken: I didn't manage any of that. When it came, the shit, it came from left field. It came in a shape and form I could never have anticipated. Of course it did, it was always going to. It always *has* done.

The symptoms of adolescent malaise have remained constant for generations. Rebellion that stems from the irrepressible *need* to question the perceived wisdom of their elders; a refusal born of the paralysing fear of messing up; a dread of standing out from the crowd for all the wrong reasons. The relentless ability of even the *noisiest* of our kids to remain resolutely *taciturn* on anything remotely emotional, except to go so far as to mutter, 'You don't get it.'

Time after time, we believe we *do* get it. We've been there, after all; we remember. Trouble is, what we're remembering is the emotional soundtrack of this stuff – the tune. But in the intervening years, the *words* – the detail, the pressures, the expectations, the *shit* – have become unrecognisable. For those with the misfortune to find themselves fifteen years of age today, it's a different world than it was back in 1975, 1985 . . .

All you can do is hold your nerve, but it doesn't feel enough, does it? Keep telling them: *I love you. You're lovely. You've got this. Breathe, eat, sleep, rest . . . It won't always feel like this.* Say it even when you think they're not listening – especially then. And know something else: 'twas ever thus. Seriously, that cacophonous clash between the ruling adult and the emerging adult has *always* played out this way.

> *Youth were never more sawcie, yea never more savagely saucie. . . the ancient are scorned, the honourable are contemned, the magistrate is not dreaded.*
>
> The Revd Thomas Barnes, St Margaret's Church, London, 1624

We need no translation, do we? 'Sawcie' youth: scornful, contemptuous, fearless, door-slamming, unpredictable, untameable, *fabulous* youth. Because however infuriating it is to live under the same roof as all that, in fact 'sawcieness' is what makes the world go round. We know this; we feel it in our *bones*. Stop screaming 'While you're under my roof . . .' at them for a moment, and we know that *some* of what's making them rage may actually *need* raging against. Their righteous indignation may actually be, in part, *righteous*. We want to cherish and nurture this energy, this courage; this dissatisfaction with 'settling'. We want them to question, to push forward, to demand that things are *right*. And yet, those very qualities can be *so* hard to live with, that we mistake it. For indolence, obstinacy, egotism.

And it really was always thus . . .

Indulge me, for a moment, in a ninth-century tale of teen rebellion on a fabulous scale. The protagonist is a teenager named Joan Anglicus, who lived in Mainz, Germany. With a razor-sharp intellect that singled her out from an early age, Joan raged, *raged*, against the contemporary wisdom that saw an educated woman as an abomination to be scorned, feared and persecuted. But she was having none of it. So on the brink of womanhood, she came up with a cunning plan. She cropped her locks, cast off female dress for male and headed to the anonymity of neighbouring Belgium, where she took the name 'John' and joined the local monastery.

Clerical robes hid Joan's curves, and she saw as an additional stroke of luck the fact that monks were traditionally clean-shaven and poorly fed, keeping them smooth-skinned and lean-featured. Young Joan was canny enough to realise that this was the perfect setting for her to flout convention, rage against the machine and hide in plain sight. Crucially, within the Church, she could get herself an education and gain access to a career path beyond agricultural graft or domestic drudgery.

And it turned out she was *good* at it – really good. Polish chronicler Martin of Opava later recorded that Joan, 'became proficient in a diversity of branches of knowledge, until she had no equal . . .' She gained a reputation beyond the confines of Belgium, moving to Rome, where she began climbing the clerical ranks: notary to the Curia, Cardinal and finally, miraculously, becoming Pope John.

Joan's story was immortalised by more than five hundred medieval chroniclers but the Catholic Church maintains she is nothing but a medieval urban myth. Advocates of Joan's story point out that the Church *would* remain resolutely in denial: Pope Joan was a *MASSIVE* embarrassment to the Vatican at a particularly volatile time when women were already rocking the papal boat. That all-girl medieval rock 'n' roll came in the form of the Mystics, a predominantly female movement claiming to have a Heavenly Hot Line and a Divine assurance that they had no need for the Church. Women, the Vatican was fast concluding, were a dangerous sex; the last thing they needed was a Papal imposter with the wrong set of genitals.

And so Joanites claim, all evidence of her existence was quietly buried. It's entirely feasible. History is replete with examples of ambitious, rebellious women cross-dressing in order to get ahead (in fact, the Church was perfectly happy to canonise one, Sainte Jean d'Arc). And the ninth-century Church had no shortage of intrigue or scandal: the papal seat was largely a political one and clerical power struggles saw 12-year-old popes and at least one 5-year-old archbishop.

Pope Joan's story didn't end well – hardly surprising, all things considered. During the third year of the papacy of Pope 'John', on a routine walkabout on the Via Sacra in Rome, suddenly the Pontiff was taken violently ill. As concerned clerics gathered round, the source of the Papal discomfort soon became apparent: the Pope was in labour. Here, the chroniclers disagree. Some claim Joan died in childbirth, right there on the Via Sacra. Others say she was deposed, served penance in a convent for many years and that her child, a son, went on to climb the ranks of the Church as his remarkable mother had done before him. Others, grimly, see her tied by her ankles to a horse, paraded through the streets of Rome and finally stoned to death by an angry, jeering crowd. Whichever way you look, the days of the *Papissa* were numbered and, twelve centuries on, are still a long way off being repeated.

There's a particularly glorious codicil to this tale. It is widely claimed by numerous sources that for centuries after the ninth-century reign of Pope Joan (in fact, until well into the seventeenth century), a newly appointed pontiff would be subjected to a particularly uneasy ritual.

A new pope would be led to the *sedia stercoraria* (literally, the 'dung chair'), where a succession of cardinals could visually and manually determine the papal gender by way of a viewing hole in the seat. Once all were satisfied, it would be emphatically declared that, *Mas nobis nominus est. Testiculos habet et bene pendentes.* ('Our nominee is a man. He has testicles and they dangle nicely.')

Outrageous myth? Perhaps. A gorgeous and eminently feasible one, nonetheless. I'd love to think Joan had the last laugh, subjecting the head of the patriarchy to a ritual testicular inspection; a tiny taste of the many indignities of medieval womanhood.

No matter where the truth lies, what's fabulous about the legend of Pope Joan is that medieval chroniclers were perfectly prepared to accept that a young girl could be so fiercely bright and unwaveringly ambitious as to rebel against the status quo, to refuse to settle for the inadequacies of the perceived wisdom of her elders, and to pull off such an audacious plan with aplomb.

For sure, centuries on and women are still fighting for full equality (not least, within the Church), but Joan's story is teenage rebellion at its finest, isn't it?

The teen rebel is not a beast to be broken and tamed, it just needs to learn focus, direction and tenacity. It needs to understand the system from the inside, in order to learn how best to help it evolve, progress. And it must have the courage to stay the course and the stamina to keep the creativity alive in the meantime.

It's worth adding that somewhere in the Vatican museum is an ancient purple marble throne, with a small hole carved into its seat.

Go, Joan!

SO . . .

The teen years have *always* been a hard tune to hum, but today's lyrics are harder than ever. Gender, sexuality . . . these have well and truly come to dominate *everything* now, written large in unforgiving neon. The thing is, you've done the groundwork. You've laid solid foundations in their early years: the stuff about mutual respect and self-worth. That's their value compass now – trust that it's well enough embedded to help put them back on track, where needed.

Drop in some casual discussion around body-shaming vlogs and the rise of comedians like Dapper Laughs; unpack it all in a reassuring, non-sermonic way. Offer up some nuggets of comfort; the 'We should all be feminists, bro', vibe (although don't say 'bro', you'll sound like a knob!).

These can be dark days. Much of the turmoil of these years can stem from that age-old struggle with identity. Remind them about what matters. And make the most of the chinks of daylight. Sit over a bowl of Doritos and slag off *The X Factor* together. Laugh together, a little bit and as often as you can. Daily, if you can manage it.

Listen. I know you think you're already listening, but listen a bit more. Talk a bit less. Give them time. *Listen.*

And keep your sights firmly set on the long game. We're working towards that fully rounded, fair, empathetic, generous, assertive human being you want to help them become. On dark days, remember that about 98 per cent (that's not scientifically founded, just learned the hard way) of what you say, they aren't going to hear. The only way is patience. Keep saying it, for sure, gently. Kindly. But you *have* to model it. Every day. You have to *be* the qualities you know they're going to need. *Do as I say, not as I do* just *won't* swing it.

If things get really tough – and they sometimes do, in spite of everything – you have to dig deep. I'm talking eating disorders, self-harm, drugs.

♦ Seek help, you really *don't* need to manage this alone.

♦ Keep your cool – and that can be tough when you're frightened. Such things are all an outward expression of an inner chaos so show them the opposite of that. Drama from you is never going to help.

♦ Don't judge them – keep your facial expressions, your words, your actions open, reassuring, *present*.

♦ Don't ask them *why* – they probably aren't going to be able to answer that one. Just make sure they know you're there, no matter what. You love them, they're lovely, it's all going to be all right.

♦ Don't blame – yourself, them, their mates. This stuff just happens, even in the strongest of families. Trust me, it just does. It *isn't* you. It isn't anyone; it just is what it is. And it will pass. In time, they will be strong enough to talk about the stuff they find helpful and the stuff they don't. Don't push for this conversation but invite it, nonetheless – it's incredibly important that they reach the point where they can *feel* you're able to hear it.

♦ Communicate with their school, college, GP. Keep everyone in the loop. Then take your lead from your kid: inch forward, enjoy the chinks of light, light the fire on the dark days and keep telling them. Keep saying it.

♦ There's nothing you can't fix together. Keep a lid on that voice inside you that's predicting a lifetime of chaos. That *isn't* how these things generally pan out: *this too shall pass*.

Where better to turn with all this than the late, great David Bowie? As well as embodying the eternal teenager, no one celebrates the irrepressible spirit of the teen like Bowie did. And no one can help cut through the incomparable pain of teen angst quite like Bowie.

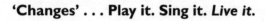

'Changes' . . . **Play it. Sing it.** *Live it.*

Chapter 20

'Rhinestone, Rimmel, and Megadeath': Self-expression, dude
Raising individuals

Vik

Recently, I was watching the HBO movie *Behind the Candelabra* about the life and loves of Liberace. For those of you under forty and unfamiliar with his work, he played piano in the 1970s and 80s, usually wearing rhinestone wings, white fur capes with 16-foot trains and arriving on stage in the most pimped-up limo you've ever witnessed. Women of a certain age swooned. Yes, of course he was gay.

My father was not gay but during the same period, he had a penchant for what might be called 'Pimp Couture'. Liberace looked like an accountant compared to him. He loved a decent pair of 'slacks' – the tighter around the arse, the better. White slip-on loafers were a big fave. On one occasion he turned up to a family party late and (reliably) pissed, sporting one shoe sans gold chain and one sparklingly adorned. Both were white; he hadn't noticed only one had the bling – 'Don't tell your mother, she'll go bleedin' mad!'

They bought matching fur 'car coats'. He returned from a sales meeting one evening and my mother cried, 'You've got *my* coat on!' Outraged and baffled, he admitted, 'I *thought* it was tight under the arms!'

'But it's got a half-belt at the back, Roy!' my mum roared, peeing herself with laughter as he recalled how many sniggers there had been around the 'Green Shield Stamps Area Team' table upon his arrival. You would have thought his colleagues were prepared for anything after he dyed his hair black and had to put make-up on his greying eyebrows and 'tash in order to match, which subsequently ran down his chin during a presentation entitled, 'You Are the Face of This Company'.

So it would be fair to say, it was unlikely any sartorial challenges from us growing teens would throw my parents into a spin. I was Number 4 so by the time I got to around twelve years old, they were knackered and basically let me juggle knives. I spent two solid years trying to be Hazel O'Connor (famous in the early 1980s): punk, perma white-faced and blacked-out eyes. Mum, cooing, shoved me into a BHS cream, batwing-sleeved, cowl-necked knitted two-piece for my nan's seventieth. But I *KEPT* the O'Connor face. Man, I wish there were photos of that somewhere! Me, wilfully miserable and terrifying from the neck up, middle-aged Avon lady down to the toes – Tim Burton, put *THAT* on screen!

But oh, my father and my elder sisters a few years before this! Despite most of his adult life looking every *INCH* like he worked in the sex industry, Dad had more than a word to say about what they were wearing and all of it around length of hemlines and amount of make-up. Yes, all of the 'You're not going out like that!' outrage, despite his own wardrobe and cosmetics addiction – he practically secreted Eau Sauvage. My middle sister now reflects, 'He was flopping his lips in vain. I just changed at my mates' if he kicked off. Thundering hypocrite!' My mum was wearing pin-stripe trouser suits à la Streisand when her pals were mostly in peach chiffon so she remained cool at the helm, looking on with a face that said 'This too will pass' and told Royston to, 'Get up and turn the telly over, for Christ's sake!', so folk could exit stage right without him noticing too much.

So I showed up in my own parenting, willing my kids to rebel – a bit, at least. I would wax on about how I raided the charity shops as an adolescent, lived in ancient winklepickers and dyed my hair with cochineal from the larder. They looked *massively* unimpressed. And, naturally, rather embarrassed by these anecdotes. So they rebelled . . . both of them. By being largely conventional throughout their teens, wearing the sort of stuff most of their tribes were wearing, and only offering me a measly *belly piercing* in return for my blistering historical coolness. Can you believe that? Utter betrayal! They had the barefaced audacity to do their own thing and I had to stand by and watch it happen, largely powerless, with just an increasingly tinny and desperate 'Could you just *consider* wearing laddered tights and monkey boots, darling? For Mummy?'

But of course a part of me (and the whole of their dad) was relieved that they weren't filthy or campaigning to be a walking urban art exhibit, plastered with illegal tatts. Our parental fear drives a narrative that chips away, irrationally, saying, 'If they go Goth, they'll go downhill.' As an educator, I had worked with kids whose outer apparel and painted faces were definitely a reflection of the misery and pain they were currently in. It wasn't always a natural, happy surge towards identity and individuality. But mostly it WAS that – an opposition to what parents thought, and a stand against the ideas and interests of other tribes of peers, a way of belonging; individuality through similarity. Or just having an enormous amount of fun with clothes and make-up and trying different versions of themselves on for a spell, while they are working it all out.

Recognising the difference between a kid in struggle and a kid in a safe amount of leather, being able to lean in and keep that conversation going along lines *other* than 'What the HELL do you look like?', that was the hard bit . . .

It's 2001. I am working with a 15-year-old girl called Tash. Except I'm not because she hasn't been deemed to have 'additional social and emotional needs', I've just had my eye on her in classes where I have been to support other kids. She's all at once brazen and then, suddenly, tiny and timid. In French, she's almost lewd in how she draws the boys in with her pronunciation. She toys with them, flicks her long auburn hair with all the precision and purpose of a Parisian. The other girls move between awe and adulation but increasingly, as Tash's take on the uniform becomes increasingly adult, they start to move away.

I knew nothing about her because she wasn't 'special' and yet she was on my mind more and more. So I talked to members of the team over a Tuesday slice of Australian Crunch with Chocolate Custard (you get your kicks where you can in Education). One of the team, Marge, a robust, warm and hilarious teaching assistant from Newcastle, arrives with her green plastic bowlful, plonking down on her chair – 'You talking 'bout Tash Moriss in Year 10? Bugger me, I know her mother, WHAT a piece of work!'

She goes on to tell us about Jules Moriss, a recent divorcée, who is into 'extreme nutrition' and fitness. With kids in the same tutor group, Marge just happened to be at a parent thing at the home of one of the other mums, and Jules rocked up: 'She took one look at me, right up and down, kissed me on the cheek pityingly and told me she still had room on her Health Boot Camp at half term, which would be super-convenient for me, what with me being a *helper* at school and all. I am THAT close to telling her to piss right off, but I didn't want to upset Cheryl in her own home and the food was lush, to be fair. Then, she says, 'I've got Tash booked in for it too. Working on her body and clothes at the same time!' I nearly punched her in the face when she said that – 'What's Tash, a size six, dya think?'

Fast-forward a year: GCSE time. I'm invigilating and I smile when I see Tash arrive at the back of the school hall. She is toned down today on the uniform front but strident in her chunky black-sandals-and-braces-clad grin. Over winter, she wore an enormous men's army coat and when she could get away with it with her head of year, twenty-hole Doc Martens. It was a daily ritual, removing her fifteen ear piercings at the morning gate. But every member of staff did so with affection and relief.

I would love to say we swooped in as a team and empowered Tash with messages about body perfection and self-worth, propelling her towards her sixteenth year relishing her young womanhood and dressing just for her – but we didn't. Tash and Jules worked some stuff out. When Jules came to terms with the loss of her marriage and allowed her daughter to grieve for the seismic shift in her own universe, away from the gym and kale shakes, they rediscovered their connection. From Marge's intel, we learned that it was a year-long street fight for them both: 'But God love her,' said Marge with real sincerity, 'when she started eating actual food and went for a drink with us, we found out just what a rough time she'd had. She's a lovely woman – she just thought great abs were the route to love.'

Tash crept towards a different tribe in school, took up guitar and embraced the Indie music scene. She still wore incredibly short skirts, but she worked out the eternal law of fashion for women: 'Stick on opaques and you're set.'

When I think of Jules and Tash stood outside school on the night of the prom, Mum beaming with her arm around her girl, who stood splendid in black velvet and a blue backcomb, I well up at the sheer magnificence of what that little family did. How they both held their nerve and their faith in one another. And how sometimes, going Goth with yer Mam's blessing can actually save you.

> *Love is the Answer*
>
> *John Lennon*, 'Mind Games'

SO . . .

♦ Our connection with our kids is bigger than fashion. Kids who feel safe that they will be loved, regardless of choice of music or clothes, will move through this crucial period of self-discovery intact – and decidedly more interesting, probably. We need embarrassing teenage years to look back on to be fully rounded folk, surely?

♦ We don't get to choose who they are. But boy, oh boy, can we help to shape them. Remember that it's more about who you *ARE* as a parent, not what you say. Funnily enough, I am a fan of wearing what I want. I know my husband prefers some things I wear to others just as I think he looks gorg with a few days' beard and steered clearly out of the range of T-shirts with 'Vespa' and 'Lambretta' emblazoned on them (or as I like to call it 'harm's way'). But he's clean-shaven and an ageing Mod. I prefer flats. We scrub up well but we can do stereo slob. That's marriage, baby, and kids who see their closest adults expressing themselves happily through clothes while not being a slave to the notions of women's and men's mags – healthy and helpful.

♦ Here's the thing: girls and women are judged and defined by their appearance and it's what triggers all the shame and 'not good enough' that's so toxic. We are *EXHAUSTED*! Men barely have to give it a thought. But young men have the damaging notions of 'laddism' and masculinity being about never showing a moment's weakness. That's the world we live in today and here's our chance to help our kids challenge that for themselves, make their own shape within it.

♦ Amnesty International did a survey that showed that around a quarter of the UK population think a girl or woman is to blame for rape if she dresses in a way deemed to be 'unhelpfully provocative'. Yes, STILL. MESSAGE: If someone hurts or abuses you, it's their fault, not the fault of your skirt or top. There is no wooliness around this. Period. Learn 'em good.

♦ Boys need to not in any way be under the impression that there is a situation, environment or even a conversation where it's OK to behave like they are just passive slaves to their sex drive. They have no entitlement; they are mammals like women who have equal needs and desires. But they have intellect too, which is dead handy when making decisions about one's penis. When we raise feminist sons, we push out into the world men who know and understand this completely.

♦ Looking and feeling good is fun, life-affirming, sometimes important and entirely an individual's choice as to what that looks like on his/her own bod and face.

♦ Being clean is non-negotiable.

♦ If they want major piercings, ask them why it interests them. What is it about them they find attractive or intriguing? Ask in a genuine 'I am interested in your view, love' way rather than a scathingly sarcastic 'Ugh! That's permanent and you're an idiot to even want one'. What might be revealed is that they're none too sure themselves about it so maybe you will arrive at a nice cosy spot where they shrug and go, 'Yeah maybe I will leave it till next term.' Take them seriously, take the piss behind their BACK.

♦ Relationships with teens need to go beyond the observational critique and script that parenting can easily fall into. There must be boundaries – they make kids feel loved, now more than ever as they feel wonderfully or woefully unwieldly to themselves, but for God's sake, muck about with them as well as chastise them about their muck! You may not like metal, they don't like Northern Soul, you both like *Family Guy* – settle in.

These kids of ours, they need to kick back and find whatever it is that makes them walk with a spring in their step and their head held high, same as everyone else. We're going to have to give them a bit of time and space to figure out exactly what that is. So step back, hold off and listen in to Lee Dorsey's 'Everything I Do Gonh Be Funky (From Now On)'.

Chapter 21

'The Hardest Bit Is When They Get to About Thirty'
Raising a glass – the adult years

Vik

Never miss a dental appointment

Always do their spellings

Deliver on the seven-a-day

Go to all the school things.

That'll do it, right?

When they're little, so much is in your gift. Or at least you *feel* like it is, most of the time. It's all at once the best and worst bit; you feel a sense of influence and control but you also feel under massive pressure to get it right. They are still malleable, legally on your watch, YOURS . . .

When you are wading through nits, threadworms and 5 a.m. starts, you catch the odd fantasy moment – 'Yeah, but when they are continent (and possibly on another continent) I will be able to claim back some of my life. I won't be thinking about them and their needs like, constantly.'

It doesn't go *exactly* like that.

Bad news? It's sort of, um, harder. They are *OUT* there. Or not quite entirely out there, cause they can't afford to move out yet. They have started shagging. Or not. They have decided what they want to do. Or, more likely, they still have no clear idea. ALL of the panicky permutations . . . You will still be holding your nerve and you don't have much of a say, if any. I can watch *The Lion King* and openly weep because they will never be little again; we'll never be back there. How I grieve for a time when we could solve pretty much anything in their world, make everything better within an exhausted haze of Sudocrem. I *LOVE* Christmas, but when I hear Shakin' Stevens' 'Merry Christmas Everyone' I am transported to my daughter's nativity and I start to shake with a sense of loss. It's ridiculous, frankly. But it doesn't last long . . .

Good news? It's what you propelled them towards and it's a *MASSIVE* joy. You can swear openly with them and laugh at the same jokes, which, if you've done the groundwork, become increasingly irreverent. You watch the people they are becoming emerge and you will see and hear things that will make you breathless with pride: you *WILL*. You can embrace (go gently on yourself, takes time, this bit) the fact that you are no longer at the tiller and that you now get to be an observer, listener – the most invested audience. Personally, I think the 'my mum/dad is my best friend' thing is daft because we *aren't* their pals: we are their parents. But you can develop a relationship now that is more matey and that's brilliant! In fact, you *should*. Nagging, being instructional, there is no place for that now. Which if you're like me and hated that bit of parenting is a blessed relief.

Be curious, be *hugely* interested, but don't pry. At times, when you're scared for them, that can be hard, but they will reveal only as much as they need to and you can't demand any more than that. This is coming from someone who came close to pinning down their child with an anglepoise, MI5-styley, for intel. Fear makes us lose our minds, sometimes.

My kids are both in their twenties now and I confess to being terrified quite a bit of the time because of the sheer fact that they are independent in the big, bad world. But man, I *LOVE* it! Because ultimately, I love the big, bad world – I *want* them out there. We can only hope that they live their lives aligned with their values and even when they fuck up, which they will, they know how to get back up with grace and good humour, knowing they are utterly loved and that love is all that matters.

I love how we like a lot of the same music: old stuff and the new that they keep me up to date on. (No, I'm not some desperate sad act who pretends to like dubstep, I just don't believe good music stopped being made in 1998.) I love how much I miss them when they aren't here, relish it when they are, and then am a *tiny* bit chuffed when they have buggered off again. I'm middle-aged, I like my peace and there's Netflix to keep abreast of. I'm relieved that I miss them when they live elsewhere but I'm not deranged at their absence because we send each other links and laughs all the time: we are connected.

Feminism has shown up in our kids in different ways. Yes, because of their gender, of course because of that, because they have to live within this world as a man and a woman and that brings with it a unique gig. They both take a common sense and intelligent approach. Equality and respect make instinctive sense to them in all aspects of life, not just around gender, but you would get a different conversation with each of them because they are individuals. It's incredibly exciting.

I love how my girl can swoon over a new pair of boots, be massively competitive watching *University Challenge*, be outraged watching particular items on the news, spend two hours getting ready one day but then slob out with her chap, naked-faced and content in her own skin the next. I love being with her and my sister, in a family bubble of womanhood, that I never want to burst cause her aunty and me can't quite believe what a powerhouse girl we've got. I love that she wants to touch people's lives in her work, is ambitious, tender, watchful and completely hilarious.

I love how my boy has told his mates about me writing this book (I found out cause one came to see me and asked me how it's going so he doesn't know I know . . . Yet.). I love how he comforted his cousin who has a learning disability throughout the day they buried their beloved grandmother, how he sends me links to current affairs pieces that offend him as much as he knows they will me, saying, 'This is a piss take, Dave' – I love it that he calls me Dave. I love how he took a run of extraordinary bad luck and turned it into triumph and I love it when we see something on the box so funny we both come close to losing bladder control.

I see them both in all their relationships and I see two mighty fine feminists, mighty fine PEOPLE.

Ma was right: it does get harder as they get towards thirty. But like her, I relish every moment cause like her, we did a pretty good job – the rest is up to them. I'm staying tuned.

This book was completed days after the death of David Bowie in January 2016. You will have noticed we love him. He got his final word . . . and he gets ours. A song to live by: 'Fill Your Heart'.

Sources

Along the way, there have been many minds greater than ours to whose work we have turned time and again for research, enlightenment, comfort and inspiration. We heartily suggest you regard our booklist as recommended reading. These include:

Books and Articles

Adiche, Chimamanda Ngozi, *We Should All Be Feminists* (Fourth Estate, 2014).

Badinter, Elisabeth, *The Conflict: How Modern Motherhood Undermines the Status of Women* (Metropolitan Books, 2012).

Bates, Laura, *Everyday Sexism* (Simon & Schuster, 2015).

Borstein, Kate and Bergman, S. Bear (ed), *Gender Outlaws: The Next Generation* (Avalon Publishing Group, 2010).

Brown, Brené, *The Gifts of Imperfection* (Hazeldene Publishing, 2010).

—— *Rising Strong* (Vermillion, 2015).

—— *Daring Greatly: How the Courage to Be Vulnerable Transforms the Way We Live, Love, Parent, and Lead* (Penguin Life, 2015).

Castle, Jill and Jacobsen, Maryann, *Fearless Feeding: How to Raise Healthy Eaters From High Chair to High School* (Jossey Bass, 2013).

Dunham, Lena, *Not That Kind of Girl; A Young Woman Tells You What She's Learned* (Fourth Estate, 2015).

Duron, Lori, *Raising My Rainbow: Adventures in Raising a Fabulous, Gender Creative Son* (Broadway Books, 2013).

Ephron, Nora, *Heartburn* (Virago, 2008).

Foucault, Michel, *The History of Sexuality, Vols 1–3* (Penguin, 1998).

Heawood, Sophie, 'How hard is it to raise a kid on your own? Where do I begin. . .' (*Guardian*, 10 October 2015).

Hughes, Sali, *Pretty Honest* (Fourth Estate, 2014).

–– 'A Note on Internet Crusaders Against Beauty' (salihughesbeauty.com, 15 January 2014).

Keller, Helen, *Optimism (1903)* (Book Jungle, 2006. First published 1903).

Kilodavis, Cheryl, *My Princess Boy* (Aladdin, 2011).

Leakey, Mary, *Disclosing the Past* (McGraw-Hill, 1986).

McIntosh, Peggy, 'Unpacking the Invisible Knapsack' (*Peace and Freedom Magazine*, July/August, 1989, pp.10–12 – publication of the Women's International League for Peace and Freedom, Philadelphia, PA).

Moran, Caitlin, *How to Be a Woman* (Ebury Press, 2012).

–– *Moranthology* (Ebury Press, 2013).

Purves, Libby *How NOT to Be a Perfect Family* (Coronet Books, 1999).

Stibbe, Nina, *Love, Nina: Despatches From Family Life* (Viking, 2013).

–– *Man at The Helm* (Viking, 2015).

Stock Kranowitz, Carol, *The Out-of-Sync Child: Recognizing and Coping with Sensory Processing Disorder* (Perigree, 2005).

Venker, Suzanne and Schlafly, Phyllis, *The Flipside of Feminism: What Conservative Women Know – And Men Can't Say* (WND Books, 2011).

Websites

'The Everyday Sexism Project', Laura Bates: everydaysexism.com

'The Pool': www.the-pool.com

'Why More Mothers Aren't Feminist', 10 June 2009: femagination. com

Movies and TV

Boyhood (2014), starring Ellar Coltrane, Patricia Arquette and Ethan Hawke

Lilting (2014), starring Pei-Pei Cheng, Ben Whishaw and Andrew Leung

Modern Family (2009 – TV series)

Parenthood (1989), starring Dianne Wiest and Steve Martin

Steel Magnolias (1989), starring Sally Field, Shirley MacLaine and Julia Roberts

The Kids Are All Right (2010), starring Annette Bening, Julianne Moore and Mark Ruffalo

The Women (2008), starring Annette Bening and Jada Pinkett Smith

Index

Growing Up Happy
Ten proven ways to increase your child's happiness and well-being

Alexia Barrable and Dr Jenny Barnett

Available to buy in ebook and paperback

A guide to nurturing positive habits and happiness skills that will last a lifetime.

In Growing Up Happy, neuroscientist Dr Jenny Barnett, and teacher and mum Alexia Barrable describe scientifically-proven methods by which children's happiness can be boosted in just a few minutes each day.

With easy-to-use activities for toddlers through to teenagers, this book steers the reader through simple and practical ways, grounded in scientific research, to enhance children's – and adults' – day-to-day happiness.

It includes
- how practising mindfulness is possible even for your toddler
- why time outdoors helps your mental state, whatever the weather
- how singing, smiling and stroking a cat all activate your 'bonding chemistry'
- why fostering gratitude will make your teenager happier

This book will not tell you how to be a flawless parent, or how to raise perfect children, but it will give you proven and successful ways in which to make the days you spend with your kids more enjoyable, meaningful, and ultimately happier.

Growing Up Happy

Ten proven ways to increase your child's happiness and well-being

ALEXIA BARRABLE & DR JENNY BARNETT

Stress-Free Feeding

How to develop healthy eating habits in your child

Lucy Cooke and Laura Webber

Available to buy in ebook and paperback

A practical guide to feeding problems in children from 0 to 5, and how to solve them.

Using case studies and real-life examples, this book is full of sound expert advice on how best to feed your young children. It helps you understand the science, dispel the myths and see that other parents have similar concerns.

Discover:
- how babies experience tastes even before they are born
- how to recognize the right time to introduce solids
- the best foods for successful weaning
- why children often reject vegetables
- how to overcome food fussiness

With hints and tips for each stage of feeding that will help develop healthy eating patterns for life, this book will put the pleasure back into family mealtimes.

LUCY COOKE AND LAURA WEBBER

STRESS FREE
Feeding

How to develop healthy eating
habits in your child